DESIGN YOUR DESTINATION

DREAM/GOAL PLANNER

ANGELA HENDRICKSON

BALBOA.PRESS
A DIVISION OF HAY HOUSE

Balboa Press books may be ordered through booksellers or by contacting:

Balboa Press
A Division of Hay House
1663 Liberty Drive
Bloomington, IN 47403
www.balboapress.com
844-682-1282

Because of the dynamic nature of the Internet, any web addresses or links contained in
this book may have changed since publication and may no longer be valid. The views
expressed in this work are solely those of the author and do not necessarily reflect the views
of the publisher, and the publisher hereby disclaims any responsibility for them.

The author of this book does not dispense medical advice or prescribe the use of any technique as a form
of treatment for physical, emotional, or medical problems without the advice of a physician, either directly
or indirectly. The intent of the author is only to offer information of a general nature to help you in your quest
for emotional and spiritual well-being. In the event you use any of the information in this book for yourself,
which is your constitutional right, the author and the publisher assume no responsibility for your actions.

Any people depicted in stock imagery provided by Getty Images are models,
and such images are being used for illustrative purposes only.
Certain stock imagery © Getty Images.

ISBN: 979-8-7652-3529-4 (sc)
ISBN: 979-8-7652-3528-7 (e)

Print information available on the last page.

Balboa Press rev. date: 11/09/2022

Design Your Destination

You can have, be or do anything you choose! Set a course, add consistency and determination and you cannot fail! Do the things that most people won't and you will have the things that most people can't!!

**"Set your mind on a definite goal
and observe how quickly
the world stands aside
to let you pass"**

Napoleon Hill

Please read through all of the material before you fill anything in. I have included blank forms for all of the exercises in the back of this planner so that you can make copies and put them into your Dream Binder. I recommend that everyone start and keep up a Dream Binder, it will keep your goals in front of you and let you add to and subtract things on your journey.

What's in a Dream Binder?

Pictures of your dream
Plans for attainment
Motivation

It's all up to you!!

Purchase an inexpensive 3 ring binder and let your imagination fly!

Make it colorful and use it every day to keep your dreams fresh in your mind!

Supplies for your Dream Binder

3 ring binder	glue
Page protectors	stickers that pertain to your goal
Paper (all colors)	pictures (printed off the internet or
Markers	cut out of magazines)
Gel pens	
Tape	

What do you want??

Ask and you shall receive! If you do not ask you will never be shown the way. Start to ask for what you want, make it an obsession. I don't mean neglect everything else in your life. I mean make it a priority. If you ask most people why they haven't accomplished their goals in life most will tell you that they don't have time to do what it takes or other people and circumstances got in the way. To get what you truly want you must take total responsibility for everything in your life! The truth is, you are the only one that has the power to say yes or no to any situation or person, and if you make a decision that leads you in the wrong direction YOU must take total responsibility for it and change your course. Do not expect other people to change to fit your needs. **You must take charge of you!**

Write it down (What is your goal/dream)

_____

_____

_____

_____

Now you must attach a deadline to your goal/dream. If you leave it open ended the odds are you will never achieve it. The timeframe should be attainable but still make you stretch to get there.

Example......   I will lose 50 pounds in 2 days.

- Not attainable

I will lose 2 pounds in 1 month

- Attainable but doesn't make you stretch

-

"If you know how to accomplish your goal then it isn't big enough"
Bob Proctor

Deadline to accomplish my goal/dream. Put a date on it!

_____

Map your goal

Mapping your goal so you can see it on paper is an important step in getting to your destination. Think about going on a trip, if you start out knowing where you want to go but have no idea about the course you need to follow it will be a stressful trip full of backtracking, but if you have a map to look at you can go from A to B to C with certainty that you are on course to your destination. This doesn't mean that you won't occasionally have to adjust your map; adjustments are just part of the journey.

On the next few lines write down all of the things that you believe must happen if you are to succeed in reaching your goal, prioritize by giving each a number of importance.

_____

_____

_____

_____

_____

_____

_____

_____

_____

_____

_____

_____

_____

_____

_____

_____

_____

_____

_____

Now pick the top five. These are your targets. Take target 1 and write down one thing that you will do each day for the next seven days to begin hitting this target. You will find the chart below in your daily exercises and in the back of the planner. Continue with each target in this manner until it is completed and then move on to the next target, if you don't complete a task move it to the next day. This exercise isn't just getting you closer to your goal it is designed to build a habit.

Repetition! Repetition! Repetition!!

Example:

Target 1- Write a paper

Day 1 – work up my outline (45 minutes)
Day 2 – work up my outline day 2 (45 minutes)
Day 3 – find reference material on subject A (1 hour)
Day 4 – find reference material on subject B (1 hour)
Day 5 – find reference material on subject C (1 hour)
Day 6 – organize my thoughts on subject A (45 minutes)
Day 7 – organize my thoughts on subject B (45 minutes)

I suggest that you put the amount of time you will work each day, if you get done sooner, move on to the next day's activity and work for the full amount of time.

WEEKLY GAME PLAN

Target

_____

_____

_____

Day 1 objective

_____

Day 2

_____

Day 3

_____

Day 4

_____

Day 5

_____

Day 6

_____

Day 7

_____

A **habit** (or **wont**) is a <u>routine</u> of <u>behavior</u> that is repeated regularly and tends to occur subconsciously.

We all have habits. The problem comes when our habits own instead of serve us. Habits that serve us make our life, health, finances etc. better. Habits that own us tear us down and make things harder. On the following page write down any behaviors you do on a regular basis (good and bad) and think truthfully about each. Does this behavior serve me or own me? Keep in mind that good things like exercise for example can become bad habits when taken to extremes. There is a chart in each month of this planner to help you identify and track possible new habits. These can be in the form of something completely new or a replacement for habits that own you. It all depends on where you want to go.

I recommend that you try to change and replace one habit at a time. Trying to change more than one can be overwhelming and may cause you to stop the process all together.

Habit: _____

Own You_____   Serve You_____

Habit: _____

Own You_____   Serve You_____

Habit: _____

Own You_____   Serve You_____

Habit: _____

Own You_____   Serve You_____

Habit: _____

Own You_____   Serve You_____

Now take each habit and write down the positive and negative things that it does for or to you.

Example: smoking   positive   negative
                    Satisfies my craving   costs a lot
                                                Bad for my health
                                                I smell bad
                                                My teeth are yellow

Do the positives outweigh the negatives?   No
Do I want to get rid of this habit?   Yes
What are the resources that I have to help me?

Doctor, internet, supportive friends and family etc.

By doing this exercise with each habit you are taking the first step in changing it or (making it stronger if it's one that serves you).

To change any negative habit you must be consistent with the new habit until it becomes embedded in the subconscious mind, when that happens it will not take effort to continue.

Habit _____   <u>**Positive**</u>   <u>**Negative**</u>

_____   _____
_____   _____
_____   _____
_____   _____
_____   _____

Do the positives outweigh the negatives?

_____

Do I want to get rid of this habit?

_____

What are resources I have to help me?

_____

Replacement habit or action

_____

Habit _____   <u>**Positive**</u>   <u>**Negative**</u>

_____   _____
_____   _____
_____   _____
_____   _____
_____   _____

Do the positives outweigh the negatives?

_____

Do I want to get rid of this habit?

_____

What are resources I have to help me?

_____

Replacement habit

_____

SUCCESS LEAVES CLUES!

Seek out people that are doing or have what you want and learn from what they do on a daily basis. How do they dress? What time do they wake up each morning? What books do they read? The habits they have are without a doubt a huge part of their success.

The Most powerful words
"I AM"

The words "I AM" can bring roses or weeds into our life!

I AM _____.

Whatever you fill in the blank with and focus on is the direction you will head. There is a power in the universe it makes no difference whether you call it god, source or universal conscience. This power only says yes. It gives you what you focus on and believe. It doesn't matter what you want if you believe and focus on the opposite!

I am stupid....the power says yes that's true

I am smart.....the power says yes that's true

I am rich……..the power says yes that's true

I am poor…….the power says yes that's true

I am healthy...the power says yes that's true

I am sick………the power says yes that's true

You literally speak or think your reality into existence!

Small change…Big Difference

This power does not judge you it quite simply sets you on a course for whatever you believe to be true about yourself and the world. You create your own reality through the words you use and things you think.

"Change the way you look at things and the things you look at change"
Wayne Dyer

If the law of attraction dictates that we move in the direction of our thoughts then we should be very careful what we think about.

This planner is only a tool. Be dedicated to using it every day and you will see results!

Details make the difference

Write down as many details about your dream or goal as possible. This may take a while, come back to this page and add more as they come to you. Details help to cement the dream as you see it into your subconscious mind.

_____

_____

_____

_____

_____

_____

_____

_____

_____

_____

_____

_____

_____

_____

_____

_____

_____

_____

_____

_____

BEGIN WITH THE END IN MIND

Thoughts are things, you don't get what you want, and you get what you think about! Why is it that most people do not realize their dreams?? The answer is they think about what they don't want instead of what they do want. Whatever you put your attention on gets bigger.

"You are important enough to ask,
and you are important enough to receive back"
Wayne Dyer

Begin with the end in mind simply means that you know what you want and start with that image. The details on the previous page are the beginning of this exercise. On the next two pages write out a statement in the present tense of the dream or goal you have. Make it as vivid as possible. See it as if it has already happened and add feeling to the picture, if money is part of your goal make sure to be specific about the amount you want. Be specific in every aspect.

"If you aim at nothing, you will hit it every time."
Zig Ziglar

See yourself already in possession
of the things that you desire!

BEGIN WITH THE END IN MIND

_____

_____

_____

_____

_____

_____

_____

_____

_____

_____

_____

_____

_____

_____

_____

_____

_____

_____

_____

_____

_____

_____

_____

_____

_____

INSPIRED

Staying inspired takes most people conscious effort. You can have the most magnificent plans but if you lose interest or other things steal your attention away from your goal it can mean the death of your dream. This doesn't mean you can't get back on track, but what if you could avoid most setbacks by keeping your dream in your line of sight and stay inspired to keep moving each day?

Tips for staying inspired

1.   Read something motivational or Inspirational (EVERY MORNING)

Reading something inspirational each morning can set the tone for a more productive day, even just a few pages can make a world of difference. Make an investment in yourself by committing to read a certain number of pages from a book that inspires you each morning.

I commit to reading _____ pages of an inspirational book 7 days per week.

Recommended books

    Think and Grow Rich by Napoleon Hill

    You Were Born Rich by Bob Proctor

    As a Man Thinketh by James Allen

    The Power of Intention by Wayne Dyer

    The Dynamic Laws of Prosperity by Catherine Ponder

Amazon is a great place to look for these books and many others!

2.   Listen to (self help) audios in your car

The average amount of time spent driving each year is equal to seven 40-hour work weeks. Says Jurek Grabowski, research director for AAA Foundation for Traffic Safety. Imagine the impact it could have on your life if you devoted even a few hours a week to listening to material that not only inspired you but taught you what some of the most successful people on the planet have done to reach their goals and dreams. Most of the books you pick out can also be found on CD for your car, I recommend that you purchase a mixture of books and CD's. You might want to purchase the titles you love in both forms.

Daily Quote:

I have provided two of my favorite quotes for each day of this planner. I recommend that you look up your own quote that inspires you each day and write it in the space provided. This process when done every day and especially in the morning will do wonders for your attitude and will help you start to find new authors that you resonate with, you may even find yourself as I did....looking up more than one each day. Repetition! Repetition! Repetition!

Six Most Important Things

In addition to the daily objective (specifically relates to your goal) you should be writing a 6 most important things list every day, each evening go to the next day and put down important things you need to do in any are of your life. Check them off as you complete them. This will give you a sense of accomplishment!

The act of gratitude strengthens our connection to infinite intelligence. Every day write down at least 5 things that you are grateful for and go over them in your mind during your visualizing time. Feel the gratitude and say thank you.

ENVIRONMENT

Where do you spend most of your time? The answer is probably your home. It's easy to waste time at home. The most destructive time waster is usually TV, it becomes a habit to walk into your living room and turn on that "drain box". I call it a drain box because it literally drains ambition, time and success right out of your life! TURN IT OFF!!

Almost all of our behavior is habitual and the TV is no exception. It will take some conscious effort to change this habit but it can make you happier, richer and healthier. I recommend that you keep a journal of the amount of time you watch TV over the course of a week, it can be a real eye opener as to how much time you waste on the "drain box". This is a great habit to plug into the habit tracker. Sit down with a piece of paper and a pen and think of productive activities to replace the drain box habit. Reading, goal planning or better yet actively working on your goal. It can be anything that moves you in a positive direction with health, goals, business, quality time with people you love or just decluttering your home and life.

"Mind is the master power that molds and makes, And man is mind,
and evermore he takes the tool of thought, and, shaping what he
wills, Brings forth a thousand joys, a thousand ills:- He thinks in secret
and it comes to pass: Environment is but his looking glass."

James Allen

QUALITY IN-QUALITY OUT

Have you heard the saying "you are what you eat"? This means that the quality of the food you put into your body will determine your health and physical attractiveness. The same is true for the information (food) that you feed your mind. I think we all know someone that reads and watches negative news, maybe it's you. What is their (your) attitude about life? I think you would agree that it's not usually very positive or productive. Feed your mind with positive information and you will get positive results!

Tape or draw pictures that excite or move you to action!

ASK FOR WHAT YOU WANT

Write yourself checks for money that you are manifesting. Who is the check from? How much is it for? What date will it be received? Now, in the memo space write down the service which you rendered for this amount. You must be willing to pay the price for what you desire. I've included a check from the bank which holds **EVERYTHING** (THE UNIVERSE) and a blank check so that you can put specific organizations etc. I recommend that you copy and use these in your binder. Remember this is a journey, you can and should be adding and removing things from your desires and dreams. We all grow and change! Review your checks daily and visualize receiving them. Be creative!

Example:

Universal Subconscious Mind
_____   Date March 1, 2025 _____
_____

Pay to the order
of _____(Your name goes here)_____   **$ 100,000.00**
_____One hundred thousand and 00/100_____Dollars

Memo: Writing services rendered _____   *Universal Subconscious Mind*

Universal Subconscious Mind
_____   Date _____
_____

Pay to the order
of _____   **$**
_____Dollars

Memo: _____   *Universal Subconscious Mind*

Universal Subconscious Mind

_____

_____   Date_____

Pay to the order

of _____

_____Dollars $_____

Memo: _____   _**Universal Subconscious Mind**_

_____

_____   Date_____

_____

Pay to the order

of _____

_____Dollars $_____

Memo: _____

_____

_____   Date_____

_____

Pay to the order

of _____

_____Dollars $_____

Memo: _____

MONTH 1

Month 1

MONTH_____

S	M	T
____	____	____
____	____	____
____	____	____
____	____	____
____	____	____

W	TH	F	S
___	___	___	___
___	___	___	___
___	___	___	___
___	___	___	___
___	___	___	___

Month [   ]

MY GOAL FOR THE MONTH

_____

_____

_____

Check list for a successful month:

_____ I know my goal

_____ I have my goal posted on mirrors, refrigerator, in my car etc.

_____ I have my inspirational book picked out and I am committed to read!

_____ I have a motivational audio ready to play in my car.

_____ I commit to using and filling out this planner each day.

_____ I commit to reading my "Begin with the end in Mind" statement out loud each morning.

_____ I will sit quietly for ten minutes each day and visualize my goal as if it were already here.

"Discipline is the ability to give yourself a command and then follow it."
Bob Proctor

WEEKLY GAME PLAN

Target

_____

_____

_____

Day 1 objective

_____

Day 2

_____

Day 3

_____

Day 4

_____

Day 5

_____

Day 6

_____

Day 7

_____

DO THIS WEEKLY

Habit _____   <u>Positive</u>   <u>Negative</u>

_____   _____

_____   _____

_____   _____

_____   _____

_____   _____

Do the positives outweigh the negatives?

_____

Do I want to get rid of this habit?

_____

What are resources I have to help me?

_____

Replacement habit

_____

_____

Keys to success!

1. **Focus on what you want.**
2. **Reward yourself for staying on track.**
3. **Visualize yourself living life with the new habit firmly in place.**

REPETITION IS THE KEY!!!!

HABIT TRACKER

Track your habits every day

Month	Habit 1	Habit 2	Habit 3	Habit 4

Month	Habit 1	Habit 2	Habit 3	Habit 4

Feeling sorry for yourself and your present condition is not only a waste of energy but the worst habit you could possibly have. -Dale Carnegie

NOTES

Gratitude (What are you grateful for?)

1. _____

2. _____

3. _____

4. _____

5. _____

6. _____

7. _____

8. _____

9. _____

10. _____

Date [   ]   **My Goal for today**

_____

_____

"If you really want to do something   _____
you will find a way. If you don't, you'll
find an excuse."   _____

Jim Rohn   _____

_____

<table>
<tr><td>

Six most important things for today

1. _____

_____

_____

2. _____

_____

_____

3. _____

_____

_____

4. _____

_____

_____

5. _____

_____

_____

6. _____

_____

_____

</td><td>

My quote of the day

_____

_____

_____

_____

_____

_____

I AM.......

_____

_____

_____

_____

_____

_____

_____

_____

_____

_____

</td></tr>
</table>

DAILY EVALUATION

I'm not here to be average,
I'm here to be awesome

_____ I read aloud my <u>Begin with the End in Mind</u> statement.

_____ I accomplished my six most important things list.

_____ I accomplished my goal for today.

_____ I read my book for the minutes I committed to.

_____ I listened to my motivational audio.

_____ I sat quietly and visualized my goal for ten minutes.

_____ I stayed on track with my new habit

What were my success's today?

_____
_____
_____
_____
_____
_____
_____

What will I do differently tomorrow?

_____
_____
_____
_____
_____
_____
_____

Date [   ]   **My Goal for today**

_____

_____

_____

"Dreams and dedication are a powerful   _____
Combination!"
                                                 _____
                    William Longgood
                                                 _____

Six most important things for today	*My quote of the day*
1. _____	_____
_____	_____
_____	_____
2. _____	_____
_____	_____
_____	_____
3. _____	
_____	**I AM……**
_____	_____
4. _____	_____
_____	_____
_____	_____
5. _____	_____
_____	_____
_____	_____
6. _____	_____
_____	_____
_____	_____

DAILY EVALUATION

"Without proper self-evaluation failure is inevitable"
John Wooden

_____ I read aloud my <u>Begin with the End in Mind</u> statement.

_____ I accomplished my six most important things list.

_____ I accomplished my goal for today.

_____ I read my book for the minutes I committed to.

_____ I listened to my motivational audio.

_____ I sat quietly and visualized my goal for ten minutes.

_____ I stayed on track with my new habit

What were my success's today?

_____

_____

_____

_____

_____

_____

_____

What will I do differently tomorrow?

_____

_____

_____

_____

_____

_____

_____

Date _____   **My Goal for today**

_____

_____

To be the best you must be able to   _____
handle the worst.
_____

_____

_____

Six most important things for today	My quote of the day

Six most important things for today

1. _____

   _____

   _____

2. _____

   _____

   _____

3. _____

   _____

   _____

4. _____

   _____

   _____

5. _____

   _____

   _____

6. _____

   _____

   _____

My quote of the day

_____

_____

_____

_____

_____

_____

I AM……..

_____

_____

_____

_____

_____

_____

_____

_____

_____

_____

DAILY EVALUATION

*My life is constantly under construction
there is always something to improve!*

_____ I read aloud my <u>Begin with the End in Mind</u> statement.

_____ I accomplished my six most important things list.

_____ I accomplished my goal for today.

_____ I read my book for the minutes I committed to.

_____ I listened to my motivational audio.

_____ I sat quietly and visualized my goal for ten minutes.

_____ I stayed on track with my new habit

What were my success's today?
_____
_____
_____
_____
_____
_____
_____

What will I do differently tomorrow?
_____
_____
_____
_____
_____
_____
_____

Date

My Goal for today

_____
_____
_____
_____
_____
_____

"You will see it when you believe it"
Wayne Dyer

Six most important things for today

1. _____
   _____
   _____

2. _____
   _____
   _____

3. _____
   _____
   _____

4. _____
   _____
   _____

5. _____
   _____
   _____

6. _____
   _____
   _____

My quote of the day

_____
_____
_____
_____
_____
_____

I AM.......

_____
_____
_____
_____
_____
_____
_____
_____
_____
_____

16

DAILY EVALUATION

"Skill to do comes of doing."
Ralph Waldo Emerson

_____ I read aloud my <u>Begin with the End in Mind</u> statement.

_____ I accomplished my six most important things list.

_____ I accomplished my goal for today.

_____ I read my book for the minutes I committed to.

_____ I listened to my motivational audio.

_____ I sat quietly and visualized my goal for ten minutes.

_____ I stayed on track with my new habit

What were my success's today?

_____

_____

_____

_____

_____

_____

_____

What will I do differently tomorrow?

_____

_____

_____

_____

_____

_____

_____

Date [   ] **My Goal for today**

_____

_____

"If everything seems under control,   _____
You're not going fast enough"
                    Mario Andretti   _____

_____

_____

Six most important things for today	My quote of the day
1. _____	_____
_____	_____
_____	_____
2. _____	_____
_____	_____
_____	_____
3. _____	
_____	**I AM……**
_____	

Six most important things for today

1. _____

_____

_____

2. _____

_____

_____

3. _____

_____

_____

4. _____

_____

_____

5. _____

_____

_____

6. _____

_____

_____

My quote of the day

_____

_____

_____

_____

_____

_____

I AM……

_____

_____

_____

_____

_____

_____

_____

_____

_____

_____

_____

DAILY EVALUATION

"Men can starve from a lack of self-realization
as much as they can a lack of bread"

_____ I read aloud my <u>Begin with the End in Mind</u> statement.

_____ I accomplished my six most important things list.

_____ I accomplished my goal for today.

_____ I read my book for the minutes I committed to.

_____ I listened to my motivational audio.

_____ I sat quietly and visualized my goal for ten minutes.

_____ I stayed on track with my new habit

What were my success's today?

_____
_____
_____
_____
_____
_____
_____

What will I do differently tomorrow?

_____
_____
_____
_____
_____
_____
_____

Date [   ]   **My Goal for today**

_____

_____

"If opportunity doesn't knock, build   _____
a door"

Milton Berle   _____

_____

_____

Six most important things for today	My quote of the day
1. _____	_____
_____	_____
_____	_____
2. _____	_____
_____	_____
_____	_____
3. _____	
_____	**I AM.......**
_____	_____
4. _____	_____
_____	_____
_____	_____
5. _____	_____
_____	_____
_____	_____
6. _____	_____
_____	_____
_____	_____

DAILY EVALUATION

"I think self-awareness is probably the most important
thing towards being a champion."
Billie Jean King

_____ I read aloud my <u>Begin with the End in Mind</u> statement.

_____ I accomplished my six most important things list.

_____ I accomplished my goal for today.

_____ I read my book for the minutes I committed to.

_____ I listened to my motivational audio.

_____ I sat quietly and visualized my goal for ten minutes.

_____ I stayed on track with my new habit

What were my success's today?

_____

_____

_____

_____

_____

_____

_____

What will I do differently tomorrow?

_____

_____

_____

_____

_____

_____

_____

Date [   ]

My Goal for today

_____
_____
_____

Today is the beginning of whatever you want!

_____
_____
_____
_____

Six most important things for today

1. _____
   _____
   _____

2. _____
   _____
   _____

3. _____
   _____
   _____

4. _____
   _____
   _____

5. _____
   _____
   _____

6. _____
   _____
   _____

My quote of the day

_____
_____
_____
_____
_____
_____

I AM…….

_____
_____
_____
_____
_____
_____
_____
_____
_____
_____

DAILY EVALUATION

*Eventually people will realize that mistakes
are meant for learning not repeating"*

_____ I read aloud my <u>Begin with the End in Mind</u> statement.

_____ I accomplished my six most important things list.

_____ I accomplished my goal for today.

_____ I read my book for the minutes I committed to.

_____ I listened to my motivational audio.

_____ I sat quietly and visualized my goal for ten minutes.

_____ I stayed on track with my new habit

What were my success's today?

_____
_____
_____
_____
_____
_____
_____

What will I do differently tomorrow?

_____
_____
_____
_____
_____
_____
_____

DO THIS WEEKLY

How's it going? Jot down your thoughts and feelings in the spaces provided.

What are your feelings about the habit you are changing and the habit you are replacing it with?

_____

_____

_____

_____

_____

_____

_____

_____

_____

_____

Have you been able to stay on track with the new habit   YES   NO

Why?

_____

_____

_____

_____

_____

_____

_____

_____

_____

_____

WEEKLY GAME PLAN

Target

_____

_____

_____

Day 1 objective

_____

Day 2

_____

Day 3

_____

Day 4

_____

Day 5

_____

Day 6

_____

Day 7

_____

DO THIS WEEKLY

Habit _____   <u>Positive</u>   <u>Negative</u>

_____   _____

_____   _____

_____   _____

_____   _____

_____   _____

Do the positives outweigh the negatives?

_____

Do I want to get rid of this habit?

_____

What are resources I have to help me?

_____

Replacement habit

_____

_____

Keys to success!

1. **Focus on what you want.**
2. **Reward yourself for staying on track.**
3. **Visualize yourself living life with the new habit firmly in place.**

REPETITION IS THE KEY!!!!

NOTES

Gratitude (What are you grateful for?)

1. _____

2. _____

3. _____

4. _____

5. _____

6. _____

7. _____

8. _____

9. _____

10. _____

Date [   ]

My Goal for today

_____
_____
_____
_____
_____
_____

"If you're going through hell, keep going."

Winston Churchill

Six most important things for today	My quote of the day
1. _____	_____
_____	_____
_____	_____
2. _____	_____
_____	_____
_____	_____
3. _____	
_____	**I AM……**
_____	_____
4. _____	_____
_____	_____
_____	_____
5. _____	_____
_____	_____
_____	_____
6. _____	_____
_____	_____
_____	_____

DAILY EVALUATION

A winner is a dreamer who never gives up!

_____ I read aloud my <u>Begin with the End in Mind</u> statement.

_____ I accomplished my six most important things list.

_____ I accomplished my goal for today.

_____ I read my book for the minutes I committed to.

_____ I listened to my motivational audio.

_____ I sat quietly and visualized my goal for ten minutes.

_____ I stayed on track with my new habit

What were my success's today?
_____
_____
_____
_____
_____
_____
_____

What will I do differently tomorrow?
_____
_____
_____
_____
_____
_____
_____

Date [_____]   **My Goal for today**

_____
_____
FOCUS on the mountain not the   _____
obstacle.   _____
_____
_____

Six most important things for today	My quote of the day
1. _____	_____
_____	_____
_____	_____
2. _____	_____
_____	_____
_____	_____
3. _____	
_____	**I AM……**
_____	_____
4. _____	_____
_____	_____
_____	_____
5. _____	_____
_____	_____
_____	_____
6. _____	_____
_____	_____
_____	_____

DAILY EVALUATION

"WE CANNOT BECOME WHAT WE WANT BY REMAINING WHAT WE ARE."
Max Depree

_____ I read aloud my <u>Begin with the End in Mind</u> statement.

_____ I accomplished my six most important things list.

_____ I accomplished my goal for today.

_____ I read my book for the minutes I committed to.

_____ I listened to my motivational audio.

_____ I sat quietly and visualized my goal for ten minutes.

_____ I stayed on track with my new habit

What were my success's today?
_____
_____
_____
_____
_____
_____
_____

What will I do differently tomorrow?
_____
_____
_____
_____
_____
_____
_____

Date [   ]   **My Goal for today**

_____

_____

Rule #1   _____

Never be #2   _____

_____

_____

Six most important things for today   ***My quote of the day***

1. _____   _____

_____   _____

_____   _____

_____

2. _____   _____

_____   _____

_____   _____

3. _____

_____   I AM……

_____   _____

4. _____   _____

_____   _____

_____   _____

_____

5. _____   _____

_____   _____

_____   _____

_____

6. _____   _____

_____   _____

_____   _____

_____

DAILY EVALUATION

Start where you are. Use what you have.
Do what you can.

_____ I read aloud my <u>Begin with the End in Mind</u> statement.

_____ I accomplished my six most important things list.

_____ I accomplished my goal for today.

_____ I read my book for the minutes I committed to.

_____ I listened to my motivational audio.

_____ I sat quietly and visualized my goal for ten minutes.

_____ I stayed on track with my new habit

What were my success's today?

_____
_____
_____
_____
_____
_____
_____

What will I do differently tomorrow?

_____
_____
_____
_____
_____
_____
_____

Date [   ]   **My Goal for today**

_____

_____

"What's going on in the inside shows   _____
on the outside."
                                                  _____
                        Earl Nightingale
                                                  _____

                                                  _____

Six most important things for today	My quote of the day
1. _____	_____
_____	_____
_____	_____
2. _____	_____
_____	_____
_____	_____
3. _____	
_____	**I AM…….**
_____	_____
4. _____	_____
_____	_____
_____	_____
5. _____	_____
_____	_____
_____	_____
6. _____	_____
_____	_____
_____	_____

DAILY EVALUATION

YOU GOT THIS!

_____ I read aloud my <u>Begin with the End in Mind</u> statement.

_____ I accomplished my six most important things list.

_____ I accomplished my goal for today.

_____ I read my book for the minutes I committed to.

_____ I listened to my motivational audio.

_____ I sat quietly and visualized my goal for ten minutes.

_____ I stayed on track with my new habit

What were my success's today?

_____
_____
_____
_____
_____
_____
_____

What will I do differently tomorrow?

_____
_____
_____
_____
_____
_____
_____

Date [   ]

My Goal for today

_____

_____

_____

"How long should you try? Until."

Jim Rohn

_____

_____

_____

Six most important things for today

1. _____

_____

_____

2. _____

_____

_____

3. _____

_____

_____

4. _____

_____

_____

5. _____

_____

_____

6. _____

_____

_____

My quote of the day

_____

_____

_____

_____

_____

_____

I AM……

_____

_____

_____

_____

_____

_____

_____

_____

_____

_____

DAILY EVALUATION

"The best way to predict your future is to create it."
Abraham Lincoln

_____ I read aloud my <u>Begin with the End in Mind</u> statement.

_____ I accomplished my six most important things list.

_____ I accomplished my goal for today.

_____ I read my book for the minutes I committed to.

_____ I listened to my motivational audio.

_____ I sat quietly and visualized my goal for ten minutes.

_____ I stayed on track with my new habit

What were my success's today?

_____

_____

_____

_____

_____

_____

_____

What will I do differently tomorrow?

_____

_____

_____

_____

_____

_____

_____

Date [   ]

My Goal for today

_____
_____
_____
_____
_____
_____

NEVER GIVE UP!

Six most important things for today

1. _____
_____
_____

2. _____
_____
_____

3. _____
_____
_____

4. _____
_____
_____

5. _____
_____
_____

6. _____
_____
_____

My quote of the day

_____
_____
_____
_____
_____
_____

I AM.......

_____
_____
_____
_____
_____
_____
_____
_____
_____
_____
_____

DAILY EVALUATION

One day or day one.
You decide.

_____ I read aloud my <u>Begin with the End in Mind</u> statement.

_____ I accomplished my six most important things list.

_____ I accomplished my goal for today.

_____ I read my book for the minutes I committed to.

_____ I listened to my motivational audio.

_____ I sat quietly and visualized my goal for ten minutes.

_____ I stayed on track with my new habit

What were my success's today?

_____

_____

_____

_____

_____

_____

_____

What will I do differently tomorrow?

_____

_____

_____

_____

_____

_____

_____

_____

Date [   ]   **My Goal for today**

_____

_____

"You are now, and you become, what
you think about."
                    Earl Nightingale

_____

_____

_____

_____

Six most important things for today	My quote of the day
1. _____	_____
_____	_____
_____	_____
2. _____	_____
_____	_____
_____	_____
3. _____	
_____	**I AM…….**
_____	_____
4. _____	_____
_____	_____
_____	_____
5. _____	_____
_____	_____
_____	_____
6. _____	_____
_____	_____
_____	_____

DAILY EVALUATION

Life is like photography.
You use the negatives to develop.

_____ I read aloud my <u>Begin with the End in Mind</u> statement.

_____ I accomplished my six most important things list.

_____ I accomplished my goal for today.

_____ I read my book for the minutes I committed to.

_____ I listened to my motivational audio.

_____ I sat quietly and visualized my goal for ten minutes.

_____ I stayed on track with my new habit

What were my success's today?
_____
_____
_____
_____
_____
_____
_____

What will I do differently tomorrow?
_____
_____
_____
_____
_____
_____
_____

DO THIS WEEKLY

How's it going? Jot down your thoughts and feelings in the spaces provided.

What are your feelings about the habit you are changing and the habit you are replacing it with?

_____

_____

_____

_____

_____

_____

_____

_____

_____

_____

Have you been able to stay on track with the new habit   YES   NO

Why?

_____

_____

_____

_____

_____

_____

_____

_____

_____

_____

WEEKLY GAME PLAN

Target

_____

_____

_____

Day 1 objective

_____

Day 2

_____

Day 3

_____

Day 4

_____

Day 5

_____

Day 6

_____

Day 7

_____

DO THIS WEEKLY

Habit _____   <u>Positive</u>   <u>Negative</u>

                                      _____   _____

                                      _____   _____

                                      _____   _____

                                      _____   _____

                                      _____   _____

Do the positives outweigh the negatives?

_____

Do I want to get rid of this habit?

_____

What are resources I have to help me?

_____

Replacement habit

_____

_____

Keys to success!

1. **Focus on what you want.**
2. **Reward yourself for staying on track.**
3. **Visualize yourself living life with the new habit firmly in place.**

REPETITION IS THE KEY!!!!

NOTES

Gratitude (What are you grateful for?)

1. _____

2. _____

3. _____

4. _____

5. _____

6. _____

7. _____

8. _____

9. _____

10. _____

Date [   ]

My Goal for today

_____
_____
_____
_____
_____
_____

The man on top of the mountain didn't Fall there!

Six most important things for today

1. _____
   _____
   _____

2. _____
   _____
   _____

3. _____
   _____
   _____

4. _____
   _____
   _____

5. _____
   _____
   _____

6. _____
   _____
   _____

My quote of the day

_____
_____
_____
_____
_____
_____

I AM……

_____
_____
_____
_____
_____
_____
_____
_____
_____
_____

DAILY EVALUATION

"No man can get rich himself unless he enriches others"
Earl Nightingale

_____ I read aloud my <u>Begin with the End in Mind</u> statement.

_____ I accomplished my six most important things list.

_____ I accomplished my goal for today.

_____ I read my book for the minutes I committed to.

_____ I listened to my motivational audio.

_____ I sat quietly and visualized my goal for ten minutes.

_____ I stayed on track with my new habit

What were my success's today?

What will I do differently tomorrow?

Date [   ]   **My Goal for today**

_____

_____

"The big thing is that you know what   _____
you want."
_____
                Earl Nightingale
_____

_____

Six most important things for today

1. _____

   _____

   _____

2. _____

   _____

   _____

3. _____

   _____

   _____

4. _____

   _____

   _____

5. _____

   _____

   _____

6. _____

   _____

   _____

My quote of the day

_____

_____

_____

_____

_____

_____

I AM…….

_____

_____

_____

_____

_____

_____

_____

_____

_____

_____

_____

_____

DAILY EVALUATION

A smooth sea never made a skilled sailor.

_____ I read aloud my <u>Begin with the End in Mind</u> statement.

_____ I accomplished my six most important things list.

_____ I accomplished my goal for today.

_____ I read my book for the minutes I committed to.

_____ I listened to my motivational audio.

_____ I sat quietly and visualized my goal for ten minutes.

_____ I stayed on track with my new habit

What were my success's today?

_____

_____

_____

_____

_____

_____

_____

What will I do differently tomorrow?

_____

_____

_____

_____

_____

_____

_____

_____

Date _____   **My Goal for today**

_____

_____

"Goals are like magnets. They'll attract   _____
the things that make them come true."
                        Tony Robbins   _____

_____

_____

Six most important things for today   *My quote of the day*

1. _____   _____

_____   _____

_____   _____

2. _____   _____

_____   _____

_____

3. _____   I AM…….

_____   _____

_____   _____

_____
4. _____
_____
_____
_____
_____
_____
5. _____
_____
_____
_____
_____
_____
6. _____
_____
_____
_____
_____

DAILY EVALUATION

"Your time is limited, so don't it living someone else's title."
Steve Jobs

_____ I read aloud my <u>Begin with the End in Mind</u> statement.

_____ I accomplished my six most important things list.

_____ I accomplished my goal for today.

_____ I read my book for the minutes I committed to.

_____ I listened to my motivational audio.

_____ I sat quietly and visualized my goal for ten minutes.

_____ I stayed on track with my new habit

What were my success's today?

_____
_____
_____
_____
_____
_____
_____

What will I do differently tomorrow?

_____
_____
_____
_____
_____
_____
_____

Date [   ]

My Goal for today

_____

_____

_____

"**Never say anything about yourself you do not want to come true.**"

Brian Tracy

_____

_____

_____

_____

Six most important things for today

1. _____
   _____
   _____

2. _____
   _____
   _____

3. _____
   _____
   _____

4. _____
   _____
   _____

5. _____
   _____
   _____

6. _____
   _____
   _____

My quote of the day

_____

_____

_____

_____

_____

_____

I AM……

_____

_____

_____

_____

_____

_____

_____

_____

_____

_____

_____

DAILY EVALUATION

"The only limit to your impact is your imagination and commitment"
Tony Robbins

_____ I read aloud my <u>Begin with the End in Mind</u> statement.

_____ I accomplished my six most important things list.

_____ I accomplished my goal for today.

_____ I read my book for the minutes I committed to.

_____ I listened to my motivational audio.

_____ I sat quietly and visualized my goal for ten minutes.

_____ I stayed on track with my new habit

What were my success's today?
_____
_____
_____
_____
_____
_____
_____

What will I do differently tomorrow?
_____
_____
_____
_____
_____
_____
_____

Date [   ]

My Goal for today

_____
_____
"Your past does not equal your future"
_____
Tony Robbins
_____
_____
_____

Six most important things for today

1. _____
   _____
   _____

2. _____
   _____
   _____

3. _____
   _____
   _____

4. _____
   _____
   _____

5. _____
   _____
   _____

6. _____
   _____
   _____

My quote of the day

_____
_____
_____
_____
_____
_____

I AM.......

_____
_____
_____
_____
_____
_____
_____
_____
_____
_____
_____

DAILY EVALUATION

Don't let small minds convince you that your
dreams are to big!

_____ I read aloud my <u>Begin with the End in Mind</u> statement.

_____ I accomplished my six most important things list.

_____ I accomplished my goal for today.

_____ I read my book for the minutes I committed to.

_____ I listened to my motivational audio.

_____ I sat quietly and visualized my goal for ten minutes.

_____ I stayed on track with my new habit

What were my success's today?

_____
_____
_____
_____
_____
_____
_____

What will I do differently tomorrow?

_____
_____
_____
_____
_____
_____
_____

Date [   ]

My Goal for today

_____
_____
_____
_____
_____
_____

"Everything begins with an idea"

Earl Nightingale

<u>Six most important things for today</u>

1. _____
   _____
   _____

2. _____
   _____
   _____

3. _____
   _____
   _____

4. _____
   _____
   _____

5. _____
   _____
   _____

6. _____
   _____
   _____

My quote of the day

_____
_____
_____
_____
_____
_____

I AM.......

_____
_____
_____
_____
_____
_____
_____
_____
_____
_____
_____
_____

DAILY EVALUATION

Don't focus on the pain, focus on the progress

_____ I read aloud my <u>Begin with the End in Mind</u> statement.

_____ I accomplished my six most important things list.

_____ I accomplished my goal for today.

_____ I read my book for the minutes I committed to.

_____ I listened to my motivational audio.

_____ I sat quietly and visualized my goal for ten minutes.

_____ I stayed on track with my new habit

What were my success's today?

_____

_____

_____

_____

_____

_____

_____

What will I do differently tomorrow?

_____

_____

_____

_____

_____

_____

_____

Date

My Goal for today

_____

_____

_____

"Thankfully, persistence is a great substitute for talent"

Steve Martin

_____

_____

_____

Six most important things for today

1. _____

_____

_____

2. _____

_____

_____

3. _____

_____

_____

4. _____

_____

_____

5. _____

_____

_____

6. _____

_____

_____

My quote of the day

_____

_____

_____

_____

_____

I AM…….

_____

_____

_____

_____

_____

_____

_____

_____

_____

_____

_____

DAILY EVALUATION

YOU DON'T DROWN BY FALLING IN THE WATER;
YOU DROWN BY STAYING THERE.

_____ I read aloud my <u>Begin with the End in Mind</u> statement.

_____ I accomplished my six most important things list.

_____ I accomplished my goal for today.

_____ I read my book for the minutes I committed to.

_____ I listened to my motivational audio.

_____ I sat quietly and visualized my goal for ten minutes.

_____ I stayed on track with my new habit

What were my success's today?
_____
_____
_____
_____
_____
_____
_____

What will I do differently tomorrow?
_____
_____
_____
_____
_____
_____
_____

DO THIS WEEKLY

How's it going? Jot down your thoughts and feelings in the spaces provided.

What are your feelings about the habit you are changing and the habit you are replacing it with?

_____

_____

_____

_____

_____

_____

_____

_____

_____

_____

Have you been able to stay on track with the new habit   YES   NO

Why?

_____

_____

_____

_____

_____

_____

_____

_____

_____

_____

WEEKLY GAME PLAN

Target

_____

_____

_____

Day 1 objective

_____

Day 2

_____

Day 3

_____

Day 4

_____

Day 5

_____

Day 6

_____

Day 7

_____

DO THIS WEEKLY

Habit _____   <u>Positive</u>   <u>Negative</u>

                                                     _____   _____

_____   _____

_____   _____

_____   _____

_____   _____

Do the positives outweigh the negatives?

_____

Do I want to get rid of this habit?

_____

What are resources I have to help me?

_____

Replacement habit

_____

_____

Keys to success!

1. **Focus on what you want.**
2. **Reward yourself for staying on track.**
3. **Visualize yourself living life with the new habit firmly in place.**

REPETITION IS THE KEY!!!!

NOTES

Gratitude (What are you grateful for?)

1. _____

2. _____

3. _____

4. _____

5. _____

6. _____

7. _____

8. _____

9. _____

10. _____

Date

My Goal for today

_____
_____
_____
_____
_____
_____

IF YOU WANT TO SUCCEED FOCUS ON CHANGING YOURSELF, NOT OTHERS.

Six most important things for today

1. _____
   _____
   _____

2. _____
   _____
   _____

3. _____
   _____
   _____

4. _____
   _____
   _____

5. _____
   _____
   _____

6. _____
   _____
   _____

My quote of the day

_____
_____
_____
_____
_____
_____

I AM…….

_____
_____
_____
_____
_____
_____
_____
_____
_____
_____

DAILY EVALUATION

DOUBT KILLS MORE DREAMS THAN FAILURE EVER WILL

_____ I read aloud my <u>Begin with the End in Mind</u> statement.

_____ I accomplished my six most important things list.

_____ I accomplished my goal for today.

_____ I read my book for the minutes I committed to.

_____ I listened to my motivational audio.

_____ I sat quietly and visualized my goal for ten minutes.

_____ I stayed on track with my new habit

What were my success's today?

_____

_____

_____

_____

_____

_____

_____

What will I do differently tomorrow?

_____

_____

_____

_____

_____

_____

_____

Date [   ]   **My Goal for today**

_____
_____
Two things you are in total control of   _____
in your Are your attitude & your effort.   _____
_____
_____

Six most important things for today

1. _____
_____
_____

2. _____
_____
_____

3. _____
_____
_____

4. _____
_____
_____

5. _____
_____
_____

6. _____
_____
_____

My quote of the day

_____
_____
_____
_____
_____
_____

I AM…….

_____
_____
_____
_____
_____
_____
_____
_____
_____
_____

DAILY EVALUATION

"Abundance is not something we acquire. It is something we tune into."
Wayne Dyer

_____ I read aloud my <u>Begin with the End in Mind</u> statement.

_____ I accomplished my six most important things list.

_____ I accomplished my goal for today.

_____ I read my book for the minutes I committed to.

_____ I listened to my motivational audio.

_____ I sat quietly and visualized my goal for ten minutes.

_____ I stayed on track with my new habit

What were my success's today?
_____
_____
_____
_____
_____
_____
_____

What will I do differently tomorrow?
_____
_____
_____
_____
_____
_____
_____

Date [   ]   **My Goal for today**

_____
_____
"Successful people are simply those   _____
with successful habits."   _____
                          Brian Tracy   _____
_____

Six most important things for today	My quote of the day
1. _____	_____
_____	_____
_____	_____
2. _____	_____
_____	_____
_____	_____
3. _____	
_____	**I AM……**
_____	_____
4. _____	_____
_____	_____
_____	_____
5. _____	_____
_____	_____
_____	_____
6. _____	_____
_____	_____
_____	_____

68

DAILY EVALUATION

The best view comes after the hardest climb

_____ I read aloud my <u>Begin with the End in Mind</u> statement.

_____ I accomplished my six most important things list.

_____ I accomplished my goal for today.

_____ I read my book for the minutes I committed to.

_____ I listened to my motivational audio.

_____ I sat quietly and visualized my goal for ten minutes.

_____ I stayed on track with my new habit

What were my success's today?

_____

_____

_____

_____

_____

_____

_____

What will I do differently tomorrow?

_____

_____

_____

_____

_____

_____

_____

Date [   ]   **My Goal for today**

_____

_____

"What ever we expect with confidence   _____
Becomes our own self-fulfilling   _____
prophecy"

_____

Brian Tracy   _____

Six most important things for today   *My quote of the day*

1. _____   _____

_____   _____

_____   _____

2. _____   _____

_____   _____

_____   _____

3. _____

_____   I AM.......

_____

_____

4. _____

_____   _____

_____   _____

_____

5. _____

_____   _____

_____   _____

_____

6. _____   _____

_____   _____

_____   _____

DAILY EVALUATION

"Whatever you are, be a good one."
Abraham Lincoln

_____ I read aloud my <u>Begin with the End in Mind</u> statement.

_____ I accomplished my six most important things list.

_____ I accomplished my goal for today.

_____ I read my book for the minutes I committed to.

_____ I listened to my motivational audio.

_____ I sat quietly and visualized my goal for ten minutes.

_____ I stayed on track with my new habit

What were my success's today?

_____
_____
_____
_____
_____
_____
_____

What will I do differently tomorrow?

_____
_____
_____
_____
_____
_____
_____

Date [   ]   **My Goal for today**

_____

_____

**Accept no one's definition of your life;   _____
define yourself.**
_____

_____

_____

Six most important things for today	My quote of the day
1. _____	_____
_____	_____
_____	_____
2. _____	_____
_____	_____
_____	_____
3. _____	
_____	**I AM……**
_____	_____
4. _____	_____
_____	_____
_____	_____
5. _____	_____
_____	_____
_____	_____
6. _____	_____
_____	_____
_____	_____

DAILY EVALUATION

"If a man neglects education, he walks lame to the end of his life."
Plato

_____ I read aloud my <u>Begin with the End in Mind</u> statement.

_____ I accomplished my six most important things list.

_____ I accomplished my goal for today.

_____ I read my book for the minutes I committed to.

_____ I listened to my motivational audio.

_____ I sat quietly and visualized my goal for ten minutes.

_____ I stayed on track with my new habit

What were my success's today?

_____

_____

_____

_____

_____

_____

_____

What will I do differently tomorrow?

_____

_____

_____

_____

_____

_____

_____

Date [   ]   **My Goal for today**

_____

_____

"There is no such thing as failure.   _____
There are Only results."
_____
Tony Robbins
_____

_____

Six most important things for today	_My quote of the day_
1. _____	_____
_____	_____
_____	_____
2. _____	_____
_____	_____
_____	_____
3. _____	
_____	I AM…….
_____	_____
4. _____	_____
_____	_____
_____	_____
5. _____	_____
_____	_____
_____	_____
6. _____	_____
_____	_____
_____	_____

DAILY EVALUATION

Be STRONGER than your excuses!

_____ I read aloud my <u>Begin with the End in Mind</u> statement.

_____ I accomplished my six most important things list.

_____ I accomplished my goal for today.

_____ I read my book for the minutes I committed to.

_____ I listened to my motivational audio.

_____ I sat quietly and visualized my goal for ten minutes.

_____ I stayed on track with my new habit

What were my success's today?

_____

_____

_____

_____

_____

_____

_____

What will I do differently tomorrow?

_____

_____

_____

_____

_____

_____

_____

Date [   ]   **My Goal for today**

_____

_____

"It always seems impossible until it's   _____
done"

                    Nelson Mandela   _____

                                           _____

                                           _____

Six most important things for today	My quote of the day
1. _____ _____ _____ 2. _____ _____ _____ 3. _____ _____ _____ 4. _____ _____ _____ 5. _____ _____ _____ 6. _____ _____ _____	_____ _____ _____ _____ _____ _____ **I AM…….** _____ _____ _____ _____ _____ _____ _____ _____ _____ _____

DAILY EVALUATION

FAILURE IS NOT THE OPPOSITE OF SUCCESS.
IT IS PART OF SUCCESS!

_____ I read aloud my Begin with the End in Mind statement.

_____ I accomplished my six most important things list.

_____ I accomplished my goal for today.

_____ I read my book for the minutes I committed to.

_____ I listened to my motivational audio.

_____ I sat quietly and visualized my goal for ten minutes.

_____ I stayed on track with my new habit

What were my success's today?

_____
_____
_____
_____
_____
_____
_____

What will I do differently tomorrow?

_____
_____
_____
_____
_____
_____
_____

DO THIS WEEKLY

How's it going? Jot down your thoughts and feelings in the spaces provided.

What are your feelings about the habit you are changing and the habit you are replacing it with?

_____

_____

_____

_____

_____

_____

_____

_____

_____

_____

Have you been able to stay on track with the new habit   YES   NO

Why?

_____

_____

_____

_____

_____

_____

_____

_____

_____

_____

WEEKLY GAME PLAN

Target

_____

_____

_____

Day 1 objective

_____

Day 2

_____

Day 3

_____

Day 4

_____

Day 5

_____

Day 6

_____

Day 7

_____

DO THIS WEEKLY

Habit _____   <u>Positive</u>   <u>Negative</u>

                                     _____   _____

                                     _____   _____

                                     _____   _____

                                     _____   _____

                                     _____   _____

Do the positives outweigh the negatives?

_____

Do I want to get rid of this habit?

_____

What are resources I have to help me?

_____

Replacement habit

_____

_____

Keys to success!

1. **Focus on what you want.**
2. **Reward yourself for staying on track.**
3. **Visualize yourself living life with the new habit firmly in place.**

REPETITION IS THE KEY!!!!

NOTES

Gratitude (What are you grateful for?)

1. _____

2. _____

3. _____

4. _____

5. _____

6. _____

7. _____

8. _____

9. _____

10. _____

Date [   ]   **My Goal for today**

_____
_____
Believe! Achieve! Succeed!   _____
_____
_____
_____

Six most important things for today	My quote of the day

Six most important things for today

1. _____
   _____
   _____

2. _____
   _____
   _____

3. _____
   _____
   _____

4. _____
   _____
   _____

5. _____
   _____
   _____

6. _____
   _____
   _____

My quote of the day

_____
_____
_____
_____
_____

I AM.......

_____
_____
_____
_____
_____
_____
_____
_____
_____
_____
_____
_____

DAILY EVALUATION

"If your ship doesn't come in, swim out to it."
Jonathan Winters

_____ I read aloud my <u>Begin with the End in Mind</u> statement.

_____ I accomplished my six most important things list.

_____ I accomplished my goal for today.

_____ I read my book for the minutes I committed to.

_____ I listened to my motivational audio.

_____ I sat quietly and visualized my goal for ten minutes.

_____ I stayed on track with my new habit

What were my success's today?
_____
_____
_____
_____
_____
_____
_____

What will I do differently tomorrow?
_____
_____
_____
_____
_____
_____
_____

Date [   ] **My Goal for today**

_____

_____

"People with goals succeed because   _____
they know where they are going."
_____
                                Earl Nightingale
_____

_____

Six most important things for today	*My quote of the day*

1. _____

_____

_____

2. _____

_____

_____

3. _____

_____

_____

4. _____

_____

_____

5. _____

_____

_____

6. _____

_____

_____

Six most important things for today

1. _____

_____

_____

2. _____

_____

_____

3. _____

_____

_____

4. _____

_____

_____

5. _____

_____

_____

6. _____

_____

_____

My quote of the day

_____

_____

_____

_____

_____

_____

I AM…….

_____

_____

_____

_____

_____

_____

_____

_____

_____

_____

_____

DAILY EVALUATION

*"It doesn't matter where you are coming from. All
that matters is where you are going!"*
Brian Tracy

_____ I read aloud my <u>Begin with the End in Mind</u> statement.

_____ I accomplished my six most important things list.

_____ I accomplished my goal for today.

_____ I read my book for the minutes I committed to.

_____ I listened to my motivational audio.

_____ I sat quietly and visualized my goal for ten minutes.

_____ I stayed on track with my new habit

What were my success's today?

_____
_____
_____
_____
_____
_____
_____

What will I do differently tomorrow?

_____
_____
_____
_____
_____
_____
_____

Date [   ]   **My Goal for today**

_____
_____
"The way I see it, if you want the   _____
rainbow you have to put up with the   _____
rain."   _____
                                Dolly Parton   _____

┌─────────────────────────────────┐   ┌─────────────────────────────────┐
│ Six most important things for today │   │ *My quote of the day*   │
│   │   │   │
│ 1. _____   │   │ _____ │
│   _____   │   │ _____ │
│   _____   │   │ _____ │
│   │   │ _____ │
│ 2. _____   │   │ _____ │
│   _____   │   │ _____ │
│   _____   │   │   │
│   │   └─────────────────────────────────┘
│ 3. _____   │
│   _____   │   ┌─────────────────────────────────┐
│   _____   │   │ I AM…….   │
│   │   │   │
│ 4. _____   │   │ _____ │
│   _____   │   │ _____ │
│   _____   │   │ _____ │
│   │   │ _____ │
│ 5. _____   │   │ _____ │
│   _____   │   │ _____ │
│   _____   │   │ _____ │
│   │   │ _____ │
│ 6. _____   │   │ _____ │
│   _____   │   │ _____ │
│   _____   │   │ _____ │
└─────────────────────────────────┘   └─────────────────────────────────┘

DAILY EVALUATION

SUCCESS IS NOT FINAL—FAILURE IS NOT FATAL
IT IS THE COURAGE TO CONTINUE THAT COUNTS

_____ I read aloud my <u>Begin with the End in Mind</u> statement.

_____ I accomplished my six most important things list.

_____ I accomplished my goal for today.

_____ I read my book for the minutes I committed to.

_____ I listened to my motivational audio.

_____ I sat quietly and visualized my goal for ten minutes.

_____ I stayed on track with my new habit

What were my success's today?

_____

_____

_____

_____

_____

_____

_____

What will I do differently tomorrow?

_____

_____

_____

_____

_____

_____

_____

DO THIS WEEKLY

Habit _____   <u>Positive</u>   <u>Negative</u>

_____   _____

_____   _____

_____   _____

_____   _____

_____   _____

Do the positives outweigh the negatives?

_____

Do I want to get rid of this habit?

_____

What are resources I have to help me?

_____

Replacement habit

_____

_____

Keys to success!

1. **Focus on what you want.**
2. **Reward yourself for staying on track.**
3. **Visualize yourself living life with the new habit firmly in place.**

NOTES

Gratitude (What are you grateful for?)

1. _____

2. _____

3. _____

4. _____

5. _____

6. _____

7. _____

8. _____

9. _____

10. _____

Date _____

Monthly Reflection

What do you think went right this month?

What do you think went wrong?

Are your positive habits becoming easier?

Write down anything that will help you make better choices.

Make adjustments to your plan.

_____

_____

_____

_____

_____

_____

_____

_____

_____

_____

_____

_____

_____

_____

_____

_____

_____

_____

_____

MONTH 2

Month 2

MONTH_____

S	M	T
___	___	___
___	___	___
___	___	___
___	___	___
___	___	___

	W	TH	F	S
___	___	___	___	___
___	___	___	___	
___	___	___	___	
___	___	___	___	
___	___	___	___	

Month ☐

MY GOAL FOR THE MONTH

_____

_____

_____

Check list for a successful month:

_____ I know my goal

_____ I have my goal posted on mirrors, refrigerator, in my car etc.

_____ I have my inspirational book picked out and I am committed to read!

_____ I have a motivational audio ready to play in my car.

_____ I commit to using and filling out this planner each day.

_____ I commit to reading my "Begin with the end in Mind" statement out loud each morning.

_____ I will sit quietly for ten minutes each day and visualize my goal as if it were already here.

"Discipline is the ability to give yourself
a command and then follow it."
Bob Proctor

WEEKLY GAME PLAN

Target

_____

_____

_____

Day 1 objective

_____

Day 2

_____

Day 3

_____

Day 4

_____

Day 5

_____

Day 6

_____

Day 7

_____

DO THIS WEEKLY

Habit _____   Positive   Negative

_____   _____

_____   _____

_____   _____

_____   _____

_____   _____

Do the positives outweigh the negatives?

_____

Do I want to get rid of this habit?

_____

What are resources I have to help me?

_____

Replacement habit

_____

_____

Keys to success!

    Focus on what you want.
    Reward yourself for staying on track.
    Visualize yourself living life with the new habit firmly in place.

REPETITION IS THE KEY!!!!

HABIT TRACKER

Track your habits every day

Month	Habit 1	Habit 2	Habit 3	Habit 4

Month	Habit 1	Habit 2	Habit 3	Habit 4

Feeling sorry for yourself and your present condition is not only a waste of energy but the worst habit you could possibly have. -Dale Carnegie

NOTES

Gratitude (What are you grateful for?)

1. _____

2. _____

3. _____

4. _____

5. _____

6. _____

7. _____

8. _____

9. _____

10. _____

Date

My Goal for today

_____
_____
_____
_____
_____
_____

"It isn't what the book costs; it's what it will cost you if you don't read it."

Jim Rohn

Six most important things for today

1. _____
   _____
   _____

2. _____
   _____
   _____

3. _____
   _____
   _____

4. _____
   _____
   _____

5. _____
   _____
   _____

6. _____
   _____
   _____

My quote of the day

_____
_____
_____
_____
_____

I AM.......

_____
_____
_____
_____
_____
_____
_____
_____
_____
_____

DAILY EVALUATION

If you never know FAILURE,
you will never know SUCCESS!

_____ I read aloud my <u>Begin with the End in Mind</u> statement.

_____ I accomplished my six most important things list.

_____ I accomplished my goal for today.

_____ I read my book for the minutes I committed to.

_____ I listened to my motivational audio.

_____ I sat quietly and visualized my goal for ten minutes.

_____ I stayed on track with my new habit

What were my success's today?

_____

_____

_____

_____

_____

_____

_____

What will I do differently tomorrow?

_____

_____

_____

_____

_____

_____

_____

Date [   ]   **My Goal for today**

_____

_____

"Dreams and dedication are a powerful   _____
Combination!"
_____

William Longgood   _____

_____

Six most important things for today | *My quote of the day*

1. _____   _____

_____   _____

_____   _____

2. _____   _____

_____   _____

_____   _____

3. _____

_____   I AM…….

_____   _____

4. _____   _____

_____   _____

_____   _____

5. _____   _____

_____   _____

_____   _____

6. _____   _____

_____   _____

_____   _____

_____

DAILY EVALUATION

"Without proper self-evaluation failure is inevitable"
John Wooden

_____ I read aloud my <u>Begin with the End in Mind</u> statement.

_____ I accomplished my six most important things list.

_____ I accomplished my goal for today.

_____ I read my book for the minutes I committed to.

_____ I listened to my motivational audio.

_____ I sat quietly and visualized my goal for ten minutes.

_____ I stayed on track with my new habit

What were my success's today?

_____
_____
_____
_____
_____
_____
_____

What will I do differently tomorrow?

_____
_____
_____
_____
_____
_____
_____

Date [   ]

My Goal for today

_____

_____

"Make each day your masterpiece"

_____

John Wooden

_____

_____

_____

Six most important things for today

My quote of the day

1. _____

_____

_____

_____

_____

_____

2. _____

_____

_____

_____

3. _____

I AM…….

_____

_____

_____

4. _____

_____

_____

_____

_____

_____

5. _____

_____

_____

_____

6. _____

_____

_____

_____

_____

DAILY EVALUATION

"Nothing is impossible. The word itself says I'M Possible."
Audrey Hepburn

_____ I read aloud my <u>Begin with the End in Mind</u> statement.

_____ I accomplished my six most important things list.

_____ I accomplished my goal for today.

_____ I read my book for the minutes I committed to.

_____ I listened to my motivational audio.

_____ I sat quietly and visualized my goal for ten minutes.

_____ I stayed on track with my new habit

What were my success's today?

_____

_____

_____

_____

_____

_____

_____

What will I do differently tomorrow?

_____

_____

_____

_____

_____

_____

_____

Date [   ]

My Goal for today

_____

_____

_____

"You will see it when you believe it"

_____

Wayne Dyer

_____

_____

Six most important things for today

1. _____

_____

_____

2. _____

_____

_____

3. _____

_____

_____

4. _____

_____

_____

5. _____

_____

_____

6. _____

_____

_____

My quote of the day

_____

_____

_____

_____

_____

_____

I AM.......

_____

_____

_____

_____

_____

_____

_____

_____

_____

_____

_____

106

DAILY EVALUATION

Whatever you decide to do, make sure it makes you happy!

_____ I read aloud my <u>Begin with the End in Mind</u> statement.

_____ I accomplished my six most important things list.

_____ I accomplished my goal for today.

_____ I read my book for the minutes I committed to.

_____ I listened to my motivational audio.

_____ I sat quietly and visualized my goal for ten minutes.

_____ I stayed on track with my new habit

What were my success's today?

_____

_____

_____

_____

_____

_____

_____

What will I do differently tomorrow?

_____

_____

_____

_____

_____

_____

_____

Date [   ]   **My Goal for today**

_____

_____

"Goals allow you to control the   _____
direction of Change in your favor."
                         _____
                    Brian Tracy
                         _____

                         _____

Six most important things for today | **My quote of the day**

1. _____   _____

   _____   _____

   _____   _____

2. _____   _____

   _____   _____

   _____   _____

3. _____

   _____   **I AM……**

   _____
                         _____
4. _____
                         _____
   _____
                         _____
   _____
                         _____
5. _____
                         _____
   _____
                         _____
   _____
                         _____
6. _____
                         _____
   _____
                         _____
   _____
                         _____

                         _____

DAILY EVALUATION

"Men can starve from a lack of self-realization as much as they can a lack of bread"

_____ I read aloud my <u>Begin with the End in Mind</u> statement.

_____ I accomplished my six most important things list.

_____ I accomplished my goal for today.

_____ I read my book for the minutes I committed to.

_____ I listened to my motivational audio.

_____ I sat quietly and visualized my goal for ten minutes.

_____ I stayed on track with my new habit

What were my success's today?

_____
_____
_____
_____
_____
_____
_____

What will I do differently tomorrow?

_____
_____
_____
_____
_____
_____
_____

Date

My Goal for today

_____

_____

"If opportunity doesn't knock, build a door"

_____

Milton Berle

_____

_____

Six most important things for today

1. _____

_____

_____

2. _____

_____

_____

3. _____

_____

_____

4. _____

_____

_____

5. _____

_____

_____

6. _____

_____

_____

My quote of the day

_____

_____

_____

_____

_____

_____

I AM……

_____

_____

_____

_____

_____

_____

_____

_____

_____

_____

DAILY EVALUATION

"I think self-awareness is probably the most important
thing towards being a champion."
Billie Jean King

_____ I read aloud my <u>Begin with the End in Mind</u> statement.

_____ I accomplished my six most important things list.

_____ I accomplished my goal for today.

_____ I read my book for the minutes I committed to.

_____ I listened to my motivational audio.

_____ I sat quietly and visualized my goal for ten minutes.

_____ I stayed on track with my new habit

What were my success's today?

_____
_____
_____
_____
_____
_____
_____

What will I do differently tomorrow?

_____
_____
_____
_____
_____
_____
_____

Date [   ]   **My Goal for today**

_____

_____

Today is the beginning of whatever _____
you want!
_____

_____

_____

Six most important things for today	My quote of the day
1. _____	_____
_____	_____
_____	_____
2. _____	_____
_____	_____
_____	_____
3. _____	
_____	**I AM……**
_____	_____
4. _____	_____
_____	_____
_____	_____
5. _____	_____
_____	_____
_____	_____
6. _____	_____
_____	_____
_____	_____

DAILY EVALUATION

"Eventually people will realize that mistakes are meant for learning not repeating"

_____ I read aloud my <u>Begin with the End in Mind</u> statement.

_____ I accomplished my six most important things list.

_____ I accomplished my goal for today.

_____ I read my book for the minutes I committed to.

_____ I listened to my motivational audio.

_____ I sat quietly and visualized my goal for ten minutes.

_____ I stayed on track with my new habit

What were my success's today?

_____

_____

_____

_____

_____

_____

_____

What will I do differently tomorrow?

_____

_____

_____

_____

_____

_____

_____

DO THIS WEEKLY

How's it going? Jot down your thoughts and feelings in the spaces provided.

What are your feelings about the habit you are changing and the habit you are replacing it with?

_____

_____

_____

_____

_____

_____

_____

_____

_____

_____

Have you been able to stay on track with the new habit   YES   NO

Why?

_____

_____

_____

_____

_____

_____

_____

_____

_____

_____

_____

WEEKLY GAME PLAN

Target

_____

_____

_____

Day 1 objective

_____

Day 2

_____

Day 3

_____

Day 4

_____

Day 5

_____

Day 6

_____

Day 7

_____

DO THIS WEEKLY

Habit _____   <u>Positive</u>   <u>Negative</u>

_____   _____

_____   _____

_____   _____

_____   _____

_____   _____

Do the positives outweigh the negatives?

_____

Do I want to get rid of this habit?

_____

What are resources I have to help me?

_____

Replacement habit

_____

_____

Keys to success!

1. **Focus on what you want.**
2. **Reward yourself for staying on track.**
3. **Visualize yourself living life with the new habit firmly in place.**

REPETITION IS THE KEY!!!!

NOTES

Gratitude **(What are you grateful for?)**

1. _____

2. _____

3. _____

4. _____

5. _____

6. _____

7. _____

8. _____

9. _____

10. _____

Date [   ]   **My Goal for today**

_____
_____
"A comfort zone is a beautiful place   _____
but Nothing ever grows there"   _____
_____
_____

Six most important things for today	My quote of the day
1. _____	_____
_____	_____
_____	_____
2. _____	_____
_____	_____
_____	_____
3. _____	
_____	**I AM.......**
_____	_____
4. _____	_____
_____	_____
_____	_____
5. _____	_____
_____	_____
_____	_____
6. _____	_____
_____	_____
_____	_____

118

DAILY EVALUATION

You can't have a million dollar dream with a
minimum wage work ethic

_____ I read aloud my <u>Begin with the End in Mind</u> statement.

_____ I accomplished my six most important things list.

_____ I accomplished my goal for today.

_____ I read my book for the minutes I committed to.

_____ I listened to my motivational audio.

_____ I sat quietly and visualized my goal for ten minutes.

_____ I stayed on track with my new habit

What were my success's today?

_____

_____

_____

_____

_____

_____

_____

What will I do differently tomorrow?

_____

_____

_____

_____

_____

_____

_____

Date

My Goal for today

_____
_____
_____
_____
_____
_____

"Life is 10% what happens to you and 90% how you react to it"

Six most important things for today

1. _____
   _____
   _____

2. _____
   _____
   _____

3. _____
   _____
   _____

4. _____
   _____
   _____

5. _____
   _____
   _____

6. _____
   _____
   _____

My quote of the day

_____
_____
_____
_____
_____
_____

I AM…….

_____
_____
_____
_____
_____
_____
_____
_____
_____
_____
_____

DAILY EVALUATION

"Don't stop when you are tired, stop when you are done."

_____ I read aloud my <u>Begin with the End in Mind</u> statement.

_____ I accomplished my six most important things list.

_____ I accomplished my goal for today.

_____ I read my book for the minutes I committed to.

_____ I listened to my motivational audio.

_____ I sat quietly and visualized my goal for ten minutes.

_____ I stayed on track with my new habit

What were my success's today?
_____
_____
_____
_____
_____
_____
_____

What will I do differently tomorrow?
_____
_____
_____
_____
_____
_____
_____

Date [   ]   **My Goal for today**

_____

_____

Rule #1   _____

Never be #2   _____

_____

_____

Six most important things for today | **My quote of the day**

1. _____   _____

_____   _____

_____   _____

_____

2. _____   _____

_____   _____

_____

3. _____   I AM.......

_____

_____   _____

4. _____   _____

_____   _____

_____   _____

_____

5. _____   _____

_____   _____

_____   _____

6. _____   _____

_____   _____

_____   _____

_____

_____

DAILY EVALUATION

The past cannot be changed, the future is yet in your power

_____ I read aloud my <u>Begin with the End in Mind</u> statement.

_____ I accomplished my six most important things list.

_____ I accomplished my goal for today.

_____ I read my book for the minutes I committed to.

_____ I listened to my motivational audio.

_____ I sat quietly and visualized my goal for ten minutes.

_____ I stayed on track with my new habit

What were my success's today?

_____
_____
_____
_____
_____
_____
_____

What will I do differently tomorrow?

_____
_____
_____
_____
_____
_____
_____

Date _____

My Goal for today

_____
_____
_____
_____
_____
_____

"Success is the progressive realization of a Worthy goal or dream"

Earl Nightingale

Six most important things for today

1. _____
   _____
   _____

2. _____
   _____
   _____

3. _____
   _____
   _____

4. _____
   _____
   _____

5. _____
   _____
   _____

6. _____
   _____
   _____

My quote of the day

_____
_____
_____
_____
_____
_____

I AM…….

_____
_____
_____
_____
_____
_____
_____
_____
_____
_____
_____

DAILY EVALUATION

Don't wait for the right opportunity. Create it.

_____ I read aloud my <u>Begin with the End in Mind</u> statement.

_____ I accomplished my six most important things list.

_____ I accomplished my goal for today.

_____ I read my book for the minutes I committed to.

_____ I listened to my motivational audio.

_____ I sat quietly and visualized my goal for ten minutes.

_____ I stayed on track with my new habit

What were my success's today?

_____

_____

_____

_____

_____

_____

_____

What will I do differently tomorrow?

_____

_____

_____

_____

_____

_____

_____

Date

My Goal for today

_____

_____

_____

_____

"Either you run the day or the day runs you."

Jim Rohn

_____

_____

Six most important things for today	My quote of the day
1. _____	_____
_____	_____
_____	_____
2. _____	_____
_____	_____
_____	_____
3. _____	
_____	**I AM……**
_____	
4. _____	_____
_____	_____
_____	_____
5. _____	_____
_____	_____
_____	_____
6. _____	_____
_____	_____
_____	_____

DAILY EVALUATION

The expert in everything was once a beginner.

_____ I read aloud my <u>Begin with the End in Mind</u> statement.

_____ I accomplished my six most important things list.

_____ I accomplished my goal for today.

_____ I read my book for the minutes I committed to.

_____ I listened to my motivational audio.

_____ I sat quietly and visualized my goal for ten minutes.

_____ I stayed on track with my new habit

What were my success's today?
_____
_____
_____
_____
_____
_____
_____

What will I do differently tomorrow?
_____
_____
_____
_____
_____
_____
_____

Date [   ]   **My Goal for today**

_____
_____
You get what you settle for!   _____
_____
_____
_____

Six most important things for today	My quote of the day
1. _____	_____
_____	_____
_____	_____
2. _____	_____
_____	_____
_____	_____
3. _____	
_____	**I AM……**
_____	_____
4. _____	_____
_____	_____
_____	_____
5. _____	_____
_____	_____
_____	_____
6. _____	_____
_____	_____
_____	_____

DAILY EVALUATION

Great things never come from a comfort zone.

_____ I read aloud my <u>Begin with the End in Mind</u> statement.

_____ I accomplished my six most important things list.

_____ I accomplished my goal for today.

_____ I read my book for the minutes I committed to.

_____ I listened to my motivational audio.

_____ I sat quietly and visualized my goal for ten minutes.

_____ I stayed on track with my new habit

What were my success's today?
_____
_____
_____
_____
_____
_____
_____

What will I do differently tomorrow?
_____
_____
_____
_____
_____
_____
_____

Date [   ]   **My Goal for today**

_____

_____

"We all walk in the dark and each of   _____
us Must learn to turn on his or her
own light"   _____

Earl Nightingale   _____

_____

Six most important things for today	My quote of the day
1. _____	_____
_____	_____
_____	_____
2. _____	_____
_____	_____
_____	_____
3. _____	_____
_____	
_____	
4. _____	**I AM……**
_____	_____
_____	_____
5. _____	_____
_____	_____
_____	_____
6. _____	_____
_____	_____
_____	_____

DAILY EVALUATION

We can't become what we want by remaining who we are.

_____ I read aloud my <u>Begin with the End in Mind</u> statement.

_____ I accomplished my six most important things list.

_____ I accomplished my goal for today.

_____ I read my book for the minutes I committed to.

_____ I listened to my motivational audio.

_____ I sat quietly and visualized my goal for ten minutes.

_____ I stayed on track with my new habit

What were my success's today?

_____

_____

_____

_____

_____

_____

_____

What will I do differently tomorrow?

_____

_____

_____

_____

_____

_____

_____

DO THIS WEEKLY

How's it going? Jot down your thoughts and feelings in the spaces provided.

What are your feelings about the habit you are changing and the habit you are replacing it with?

_____

_____

_____

_____

_____

_____

_____

_____

_____

_____

Have you been able to stay on track with the new habit   YES   NO

Why?

_____

_____

_____

_____

_____

_____

_____

_____

_____

WEEKLY GAME PLAN

Target

_____

_____

_____

Day 1 objective

_____

Day 2

_____

Day 3

_____

Day 4

_____

Day 5

_____

Day 6

_____

Day 7

_____

DO THIS WEEKLY

Habit _____   **Positive**   **Negative**

_____   _____

_____   _____

_____   _____

_____   _____

_____   _____

Do the positives outweigh the negatives?

_____

Do I want to get rid of this habit?

_____

What are resources I have to help me?

_____

Replacement habit

_____

_____

Keys to success!

1. **Focus on what you want.**
2. **Reward yourself for staying on track.**
3. **Visualize yourself living life with the new habit firmly in place.**

REPETITION IS THE KEY!!!!

NOTES

Gratitude (What are you grateful for?)

1. _____

2. _____

3. _____

4. _____

5. _____

6. _____

7. _____

8. _____

9. _____

10. _____

Date

My Goal for today

_____
_____
_____
_____
_____
_____

"Fear does not stop death, it stops life!"

Six most important things for today

1. _____
_____
_____

2. _____
_____
_____

3. _____
_____
_____

4. _____
_____
_____

5. _____
_____
_____

6. _____
_____
_____

My quote of the day

_____
_____
_____
_____
_____
_____

I AM.......

_____
_____
_____
_____
_____
_____
_____
_____
_____
_____
_____

DAILY EVALUATION

Your only limit is you!

_____ I read aloud my <u>Begin with the End in Mind</u> statement.

_____ I accomplished my six most important things list.

_____ I accomplished my goal for today.

_____ I read my book for the minutes I committed to.

_____ I listened to my motivational audio.

_____ I sat quietly and visualized my goal for ten minutes.

_____ I stayed on track with my new habit

What were my success's today?

_____

_____

_____

_____

_____

_____

_____

What will I do differently tomorrow?

_____

_____

_____

_____

_____

_____

_____

Date [   ] **My Goal for today**

_____

_____

"We tend to live up to our expectations"   _____

Earl Nightingale   _____

_____

_____

Six most important things for today   *My quote of the day*

1. _____   _____
   _____   _____
   _____   _____
                              _____
2. _____   _____
   _____   _____
   _____

3. _____   I AM.......
   _____
   _____   _____
                              _____
4. _____   _____
   _____   _____
   _____
                              _____
5. _____   _____
   _____   _____
   _____   _____
                              _____
6. _____   _____
   _____   _____
   _____   _____

DAILY EVALUATION

"When Shit happens turn it into fertilizer"

_____ I read aloud my <u>Begin with the End in Mind</u> statement.

_____ I accomplished my six most important things list.

_____ I accomplished my goal for today.

_____ I read my book for the minutes I committed to.

_____ I listened to my motivational audio.

_____ I sat quietly and visualized my goal for ten minutes.

_____ I stayed on track with my new habit

What were my success's today?
_____
_____
_____
_____
_____
_____
_____

What will I do differently tomorrow?
_____
_____
_____
_____
_____
_____
_____

Date [   ]   **My Goal for today**

_____
_____
"Your past does not equal your future"   _____
Tony Robbins   _____
_____
_____

<u>Six most important things for today</u>

1. _____
_____
_____

2. _____
_____
_____

3. _____
_____
_____

4. _____
_____
_____

5. _____
_____
_____

6. _____
_____
_____

My quote of the day

_____
_____
_____
_____
_____
_____

I AM…….

_____
_____
_____
_____
_____
_____
_____
_____
_____
_____
_____

DAILY EVALUATION

"You will never find time for anything, you must make it."
Charles Buxton. M

_____ I read aloud my <u>Begin with the End in Mind</u> statement.

_____ I accomplished my six most important things list.

_____ I accomplished my goal for today.

_____ I read my book for the minutes I committed to.

_____ I listened to my motivational audio.

_____ I sat quietly and visualized my goal for ten minutes.

_____ I stayed on track with my new habit

What were my success's today?

_____
_____
_____
_____
_____
_____
_____

What will I do differently tomorrow?

_____
_____
_____
_____
_____
_____
_____

Date [   ]   **My Goal for today**

_____
_____
"Winners make a habit of   _____
manufacturing their own positive   _____
expectations in advance of the event." _____
Brian Tracy   _____

Six most important things for today   *My quote of the day*

1. _____   _____
   _____   _____
   _____   _____
                                    _____
2. _____   _____
   _____   _____
   _____

3. _____   I AM.......
   _____
   _____   _____
                                    _____
4. _____   _____
   _____   _____
   _____   _____
                                    _____
5. _____   _____
   _____   _____
   _____   _____
                                    _____
6. _____   _____
   _____   _____
   _____   _____

DAILY EVALUATION

Your life is your story, write well, edit often.

_____ I read aloud my <u>Begin with the End in Mind</u> statement.

_____ I accomplished my six most important things list.

_____ I accomplished my goal for today.

_____ I read my book for the minutes I committed to.

_____ I listened to my motivational audio.

_____ I sat quietly and visualized my goal for ten minutes.

_____ I stayed on track with my new habit

What were my success's today?

_____

_____

_____

_____

_____

_____

_____

What will I do differently tomorrow?

_____

_____

_____

_____

_____

_____

_____

Date [   ]   **My Goal for today**

_____
_____
_____

"If you do what you've always done,   _____
you will Get what you've always   _____
gotten."
                                            _____
                        Tony Robbins

Six most important things for today

1. _____
   _____
   _____

2. _____
   _____
   _____

3. _____
   _____
   _____

4. _____
   _____
   _____

5. _____
   _____
   _____

6. _____
   _____
   _____

My quote of the day

_____
_____
_____
_____
_____
_____

I AM.......

_____
_____
_____
_____
_____
_____
_____
_____
_____
_____

DAILY EVALUATION

Don't let small minds convince you that your dreams are to big!

_____ I read aloud my <u>Begin with the End in Mind</u> statement.

_____ I accomplished my six most important things list.

_____ I accomplished my goal for today.

_____ I read my book for the minutes I committed to.

_____ I listened to my motivational audio.

_____ I sat quietly and visualized my goal for ten minutes.

_____ I stayed on track with my new habit

What were my success's today?

_____

_____

_____

_____

_____

_____

_____

What will I do differently tomorrow?

_____

_____

_____

_____

_____

_____

_____

Date [   ]   **My Goal for today**

_____

_____

"The big thing is that you know what   _____
You want"
                                            _____
                                Earl Nightingale
                                            _____

                                            _____

Six most important things for today	*My quote of the day*
1. _____	_____
_____	_____
_____	_____
2. _____	_____
_____	_____
_____	_____
3. _____	
_____	**I AM……**
_____	_____
4. _____	_____
_____	_____
_____	_____
5. _____	_____
_____	_____
_____	_____
6. _____	_____
_____	_____
_____	_____

DAILY EVALUATION

The grass is greener where you water it.

_____ I read aloud my <u>Begin with the End in Mind</u> statement.

_____ I accomplished my six most important things list.

_____ I accomplished my goal for today.

_____ I read my book for the minutes I committed to.

_____ I listened to my motivational audio.

_____ I sat quietly and visualized my goal for ten minutes.

_____ I stayed on track with my new habit

What were my success's today?

_____
_____
_____
_____
_____
_____
_____

What will I do differently tomorrow?

_____
_____
_____
_____
_____
_____
_____

Date [   ]   **My Goal for today**

_____

_____

"Be so good they can't ignore you"   _____

Steve Martin   _____

_____

_____

<u>Six most important things for today</u>

1. _____
   _____
   _____

2. _____
   _____
   _____

3. _____
   _____
   _____

4. _____
   _____
   _____

5. _____
   _____
   _____

6. _____
   _____
   _____

My quote of the day

_____

_____

_____

_____

_____

_____

I AM.......

_____

_____

_____

_____

_____

_____

_____

_____

_____

DAILY EVALUATION

Go as long as you can and then take another step!

_____ I read aloud my <u>Begin with the End in Mind</u> statement.

_____ I accomplished my six most important things list.

_____ I accomplished my goal for today.

_____ I read my book for the minutes I committed to.

_____ I listened to my motivational audio.

_____ I sat quietly and visualized my goal for ten minutes.

_____ I stayed on track with my new habit

What were my success's today?

_____

_____

_____

_____

_____

_____

_____

What will I do differently tomorrow?

_____

_____

_____

_____

_____

_____

_____

DO THIS WEEKLY

How's it going? Jot down your thoughts and feelings in the spaces provided.

What are your feelings about the habit you are changing and the habit you are replacing it with?

_____

_____

_____

_____

_____

_____

_____

_____

_____

_____

Have you been able to stay on track with the new habit   YES   NO

Why?

_____

_____

_____

_____

_____

_____

_____

_____

_____

_____

WEEKLY GAME PLAN

Target

_____

_____

_____

Day 1 objective

_____

Day 2

_____

Day 3

_____

Day 4

_____

Day 5

_____

Day 6

_____

Day 7

_____

DO THIS WEEKLY

Habit _____   <u>Positive</u>   <u>Negative</u>

                                                         _____   _____

                                                          _____   _____

                                                          _____   _____

                                                          _____   _____

                                                          _____   _____

Do the positives outweigh the negatives?

_____

Do I want to get rid of this habit?

_____

What are resources I have to help me?

_____

Replacement habit

_____

_____

Keys to success!

1. **Focus on what you want.**
2. **Reward yourself for staying on track.**
3. **Visualize yourself living life with the new habit firmly in place.**

REPETITION IS THE KEY!!!!

NOTES

Gratitude (What are you grateful for?)

1. _____

2. _____

3. _____

4. _____

5. _____

6. _____

7. _____

8. _____

9. _____

10. _____

Date [   ]

My Goal for today

_____
_____
_____
_____
_____
_____

"Don't wait for the perfect moment, take the moment and make it perfect."

<u>Six most important things for today</u>

1. _____
_____
_____

2. _____
_____
_____

3. _____
_____
_____

4. _____
_____
_____

5. _____
_____
_____

6. _____
_____
_____

My quote of the day

_____
_____
_____
_____
_____
_____

I AM.......

_____
_____
_____
_____
_____
_____
_____
_____
_____
_____
_____

DAILY EVALUATION

Be better than you were yesterday

_____ I read aloud my <u>Begin with the End in Mind</u> statement.

_____ I accomplished my six most important things list.

_____ I accomplished my goal for today.

_____ I read my book for the minutes I committed to.

_____ I listened to my motivational audio.

_____ I sat quietly and visualized my goal for ten minutes.

_____ I stayed on track with my new habit

What were my success's today?

_____

_____

_____

_____

_____

_____

_____

What will I do differently tomorrow?

_____

_____

_____

_____

_____

_____

_____

Date [   ]   **My Goal for today**

_____

_____

You attract what you are not what you   _____
want, If you want great, then be great!
_____

_____

_____

Six most important things for today	My quote of the day
1. _____	_____
_____	_____
_____	_____
2. _____	_____
_____	_____
_____	_____
3. _____	
_____	**I AM…….**
_____	_____
4. _____	_____
_____	_____
_____	_____
5. _____	_____
_____	_____
_____	_____
6. _____	_____
_____	_____
_____	_____

DAILY EVALUATION

"It's easy to be a critic, but being a doer requires effort, risk, and change."
Wayne Dyer

_____ I read aloud my <u>Begin with the End in Mind</u> statement.

_____ I accomplished my six most important things list.

_____ I accomplished my goal for today.

_____ I read my book for the minutes I committed to.

_____ I listened to my motivational audio.

_____ I sat quietly and visualized my goal for ten minutes.

_____ I stayed on track with my new habit

What were my success's today?

_____
_____
_____
_____
_____
_____
_____

What will I do differently tomorrow?

_____
_____
_____
_____
_____
_____
_____

Date [   ]   **My Goal for today**

_____

_____

"It doesn't matter where you are   _____
coming from. All that matters is
where you are going."   _____

Brian Tracy   _____

_____

Six most important things for today   *My quote of the day*

1. _____   _____
   _____
   _____   _____

2. _____   _____
   _____
   _____   _____

3. _____   _____
   _____
   _____   _____

4. _____
   _____   I AM.......
   _____
                                 _____
5. _____
   _____   _____
   _____
                                 _____
6. _____
   _____   _____
   _____
                                 _____

                                 _____

                                 _____

                                 _____

                                 _____

158

DAILY EVALUATION

Believe you can and you're half way there.

_____ I read aloud my <u>Begin with the End in Mind</u> statement.

_____ I accomplished my six most important things list.

_____ I accomplished my goal for today.

_____ I read my book for the minutes I committed to.

_____ I listened to my motivational audio.

_____ I sat quietly and visualized my goal for ten minutes.

_____ I stayed on track with my new habit

```
What were my success's today?
_____
_____
_____
_____
_____
_____
_____
```

```
What will I do differently tomorrow?
_____
_____
_____
_____
_____
_____
_____
```

Date [   ]   **My Goal for today**

_____

_____

"Never say anything about yourself   _____
that you Don't want to come true."
_____
                        Brian Tracy
_____

_____

Six most important things for today	*My quote of the day*
1. _____	_____
_____	_____
_____	_____
2. _____	_____
_____	_____
_____	_____
3. _____	
_____	**I AM.......**
_____	_____
4. _____	_____
_____	_____
_____	_____
5. _____	_____
_____	_____
_____	_____
6. _____	_____
_____	_____
_____	_____

DAILY EVALUATION

"An ounce of performance is worth pounds of promises"
Mae West

____ I read aloud my <u>Begin with the End in Mind</u> statement.

____ I accomplished my six most important things list.

____ I accomplished my goal for today.

____ I read my book for the minutes I committed to.

____ I listened to my motivational audio.

____ I sat quietly and visualized my goal for ten minutes.

____ I stayed on track with my new habit

What were my success's today?

_____

_____

_____

_____

_____

_____

_____

What will I do differently tomorrow?

_____

_____

_____

_____

_____

_____

_____

_____

Date [   ]   **My Goal for today**

_____

_____

"You'll find boredom where there is the absence of a good idea."

_____

_____

_____

_____

<u>Six most important things for today</u>

1. _____
   _____
   _____

2. _____
   _____
   _____

3. _____
   _____
   _____

4. _____
   _____
   _____

5. _____
   _____
   _____

6. _____
   _____
   _____

My quote of the day

_____

_____

_____

_____

_____

_____

I AM.......

_____

_____

_____

_____

_____

_____

_____

_____

_____

_____

DAILY EVALUATION

"The first and best victory is to conquer self"
Plato

_____ I read aloud my <u>Begin with the End in Mind</u> statement.

_____ I accomplished my six most important things list.

_____ I accomplished my goal for today.

_____ I read my book for the minutes I committed to.

_____ I listened to my motivational audio.

_____ I sat quietly and visualized my goal for ten minutes.

_____ I stayed on track with my new habit

What were my success's today?

_____

_____

_____

_____

_____

_____

_____

What will I do differently tomorrow?

_____

_____

_____

_____

_____

_____

_____

Date [   ]   **My Goal for today**

_____
_____
"Most people fail in life because they   _____
Major in minor things."   _____
Tony Robbins   _____
_____

Six most important things for today	My quote of the day
1. _____	_____
_____	_____
_____	_____
2. _____	_____
_____	_____
_____	_____
3. _____	
_____	**I AM……**
_____	_____
4. _____	_____
_____	_____
_____	_____
5. _____	_____
_____	_____
_____	_____
6. _____	_____
_____	_____
_____	_____

DAILY EVALUATION

Mistakes are proof that you are trying

_____ I read aloud my <u>Begin with the End in Mind</u> statement.

_____ I accomplished my six most important things list.

_____ I accomplished my goal for today.

_____ I read my book for the minutes I committed to.

_____ I listened to my motivational audio.

_____ I sat quietly and visualized my goal for ten minutes.

_____ I stayed on track with my new habit

What were my success's today?
_____
_____
_____
_____
_____
_____
_____

What will I do differently tomorrow?
_____
_____
_____
_____
_____
_____
_____

Date [   ]   **My Goal for today**

_____

_____

The best view comes after the hardest   _____
Climb.

_____

_____

_____

Six most important things for today

1. _____
_____
_____

2. _____
_____
_____

3. _____
_____
_____

4. _____
_____
_____

5. _____
_____
_____

6. _____
_____
_____

My quote of the day

_____

_____

_____

_____

_____

_____

I AM.......

_____

_____

_____

_____

_____

_____

_____

_____

_____

_____

_____

DAILY EVALUATION

You must do the thing you think you cannot

_____ I read aloud my <u>Begin with the End in Mind</u> statement.

_____ I accomplished my six most important things list.

_____ I accomplished my goal for today.

_____ I read my book for the minutes I committed to.

_____ I listened to my motivational audio.

_____ I sat quietly and visualized my goal for ten minutes.

_____ I stayed on track with my new habit

What were my success's today?

_____

_____

_____

_____

_____

_____

_____

What will I do differently tomorrow?

_____

_____

_____

_____

_____

_____

_____

DO THIS WEEKLY

How's it going? Jot down your thoughts and feelings in the spaces provided.

What are your feelings about the habit you are changing and the habit you are replacing it with?

_____

_____

_____

_____

_____

_____

_____

_____

_____

Have you been able to stay on track with the new habit   YES   NO

Why?

_____

_____

_____

_____

_____

_____

_____

_____

_____

WEEKLY GAME PLAN

Target

_____

_____

_____

Day 1 objective

_____

Day 2

_____

Day 3

_____

Day 4

_____

Day 5

_____

Day 6

_____

Day 7

_____

DO THIS WEEKLY

Habit _____   <u>Positive</u>   <u>Negative</u>

_____   _____

_____   _____

_____   _____

_____   _____

_____   _____

Do the positives outweigh the negatives?

_____

Do I want to get rid of this habit?

_____

What are resources I have to help me?

_____

Replacement habit

_____

_____

Keys to success!

1. **Focus on what you want.**
2. **Reward yourself for staying on track.**
3. **Visualize yourself living life with the new habit firmly in place.**

REPETITION IS THE KEY!!!!

NOTES

Gratitude (What are you grateful for?)

1. _____

2. _____

3. _____

4. _____

5. _____

6. _____

7. _____

8. _____

9. _____

10. _____

Date [   ]   **My Goal for today**

_____

_____

Believe! Achieve! Succeed!   _____

_____

_____

_____

Six most important things for today	My quote of the day

Six most important things for today

1. _____

_____

_____

2. _____

_____

_____

3. _____

_____

_____

4. _____

_____

_____

5. _____

_____

_____

6. _____

_____

_____

My quote of the day

_____

_____

_____

_____

_____

_____

I AM…….

_____

_____

_____

_____

_____

_____

_____

_____

_____

_____

DAILY EVALUATION

It's never too late to be what you might have been

_____ I read aloud my <u>Begin with the End in Mind</u> statement.

_____ I accomplished my six most important things list.

_____ I accomplished my goal for today.

_____ I read my book for the minutes I committed to.

_____ I listened to my motivational audio.

_____ I sat quietly and visualized my goal for ten minutes.

_____ I stayed on track with my new habit

What were my success's today?

_____

_____

_____

_____

_____

_____

_____

What will I do differently tomorrow?

_____

_____

_____

_____

_____

_____

_____

Date [   ]   **My Goal for today**

_____

"The mind moves in the direction of   _____
our Currently dominant thoughts"
                                                  _____
Earl Nightingale
                                                  _____

                                                  _____

                                                  _____

Six most important things for today	*My quote of the day*
1. _____	
2. _____	
3. _____	**I AM……**
4. _____	
5. _____	
6. _____	

DAILY EVALUATION

"The key to success is action"
Brian Tracy

_____ I read aloud my <u>Begin with the End in Mind</u> statement.

_____ I accomplished my six most important things list.

_____ I accomplished my goal for today.

_____ I read my book for the minutes I committed to.

_____ I listened to my motivational audio.

_____ I sat quietly and visualized my goal for ten minutes.

_____ I stayed on track with my new habit

What were my success's today?
_____
_____
_____
_____
_____
_____
_____

What will I do differently tomorrow?
_____
_____
_____
_____
_____
_____
_____

Date [   ]   **My Goal for today**

_____

_____

"Your attitude, not your aptitude, will   _____
Determine you altitude."
                                                _____
                              Zig Zigler
                                                _____

                                                _____

Six most important things for today	*My quote of the day*
1. _____	_____
_____	_____
_____	_____
2. _____	_____
_____	_____
_____	_____
3. _____	
_____	**I AM…….**
_____	_____
4. _____	_____
_____	_____
_____	_____
5. _____	_____
_____	_____
_____	_____
6. _____	_____
_____	_____
_____	_____

176

DAILY EVALUATION

"Most so called failures are only temporary defeats"
Napoleon Hill

_____ I read aloud my <u>Begin with the End in Mind</u> statement.

_____ I accomplished my six most important things list.

_____ I accomplished my goal for today.

_____ I read my book for the minutes I committed to.

_____ I listened to my motivational audio.

_____ I sat quietly and visualized my goal for ten minutes.

_____ I stayed on track with my new habit

What were my success's today?

_____
_____
_____
_____
_____
_____
_____

What will I do differently tomorrow?

_____
_____
_____
_____
_____
_____
_____

DO THIS WEEKLY

Habit _____   **Positive**   **Negative**

                                          _____   _____

                                          _____   _____

                                          _____   _____

                                          _____   _____

                                          _____   _____

Do the positives outweigh the negatives?

_____

Do I want to get rid of this habit?

_____

What are resources I have to help me?

_____

Replacement habit

_____

_____

Keys to success!

1. **Focus on what you want.**
2. **Reward yourself for staying on track.**
3. **Visualize yourself living life with the new habit firmly in place.**

NOTES

Gratitude (What are you grateful for?)

1. _____

2. _____

3. _____

4. _____

5. _____

6. _____

7. _____

8. _____

9. _____

10. _____

Date _____

Monthly Reflection

What do you think went right this month?
What do you think went wrong?
Are your positive habits becoming easier?
Write down anything that will help you make better choices.
Make adjustments to your plan.

_____

_____

_____

_____

_____

_____

_____

_____

_____

_____

_____

_____

_____

_____

_____

_____

_____

MONTH 3

Month 3

MONTH_____

S	M	T
____	____	____
____	____	____
____	____	____
____	____	____
____	____	____

W	TH	F	S
_____	_____	_____	_____
_____	_____	_____	_____
_____	_____	_____	_____
_____	_____	_____	_____
_____	_____	_____	_____

Month [   ]

MY GOAL FOR THE MONTH

_____

_____

_____

Check list for a successful month:

_____ I know my goal

_____ I have my goal posted on mirrors, refrigerator, in my car etc.

_____ I have my inspirational book picked out and I am committed to read!

_____ I have a motivational audio ready to play in my car.

_____ I commit to using and filling out this planner each day.

_____ I commit to reading my "Begin with the end in Mind" statement out loud each morning.

_____ I will sit quietly for ten minutes each day and visualize my goal as if it were already here.

*"Discipline is the ability to give yourself
a command and then follow it."*
Bob Proctor

WEEKLY GAME PLAN

Target

_____

_____

_____

Day 1 objective

_____

Day 2

_____

Day 3

_____

Day 4

_____

Day 5

_____

Day 6

_____

Day 7

_____

DO THIS WEEKLY

Habit _____   **Positive**   **Negative**

                                                    _____   _____

   _____   _____

   _____   _____

   _____   _____

   _____   _____

Do the positives outweigh the negatives?

_____

Do I want to get rid of this habit?

_____

What are resources I have to help me?

_____

Replacement habit

_____

_____

Keys to success!

1. **Focus on what you want.**
2. **Reward yourself for staying on track.**
3. **Visualize yourself living life with the new habit firmly in place.**

REPETITION IS THE KEY!!!!

HABIT TRACKER

Track your habits every day

Month	Habit 1	Habit 2	Habit 3	Habit 4

Month	Habit 1	Habit 2	Habit 3	Habit 4

Feeling sorry for yourself and your present condition is not only a waste of energy but the worst habit you could possibly have. -Dale Carnegie

NOTES

Gratitude (What are you grateful for?)

1. _____

2. _____

3. _____

4. _____

5. _____

6. _____

7. _____

8. _____

9. _____

10. _____

Date [   ]   **My Goal for today**

_____

_____

"If you really want to do something   _____
you will find a way. If you don't, you'll
find an excuse."   _____

Jim Rohn   _____

_____

<u>Six most important things for today</u>   *My quote of the day*

1. _____   _____
   _____   _____
   _____   _____

2. _____   _____
   _____   _____
   _____   _____

3. _____   I AM…….
   _____
   _____   _____

4. _____   _____
   _____   _____
   _____   _____

5. _____   _____
   _____   _____
   _____   _____

6. _____   _____
   _____   _____
   _____   _____

DAILY EVALUATION

I'm not here to be average. I'm here to be awesome.

_____ I read aloud my <u>Begin with the End in Mind</u> statement.

_____ I accomplished my six most important things list.

_____ I accomplished my goal for today.

_____ I read my book for the minutes I committed to.

_____ I listened to my motivational audio.

_____ I sat quietly and visualized my goal for ten minutes.

_____ I stayed on track with my new habit

What were my success's today?

_____

_____

_____

_____

_____

_____

_____

What will I do differently tomorrow?

_____

_____

_____

_____

_____

_____

_____

_____

Date [   ]   **My Goal for today**

_____
_____
"Dreams and dedication are a powerful   _____
Combination!"   _____
                    William Longgood   _____
                                                 _____

Six most important things for today | *My quote of the day*
                                        |
1. _____ | _____
   _____ | _____
   _____ | _____
                                        | _____
2. _____ | _____
   _____ | _____
   _____ |
                                        | I AM…….
3. _____ |
   _____ | _____
   _____ | _____
                                        | _____
4. _____ | _____
   _____ | _____
   _____ | _____
                                        | _____
5. _____ | _____
   _____ | _____
   _____ | _____
                                        | _____
6. _____ |
   _____ |
   _____ |

192

DAILY EVALUATION

"Without proper self-evaluation failure is inevitable"
John Wooden

_____ I read aloud my <u>Begin with the End in Mind</u> statement.

_____ I accomplished my six most important things list.

_____ I accomplished my goal for today.

_____ I read my book for the minutes I committed to.

_____ I listened to my motivational audio.

_____ I sat quietly and visualized my goal for ten minutes.

_____ I stayed on track with my new habit

What were my success's today?

_____
_____
_____
_____
_____
_____
_____

What will I do differently tomorrow?

_____
_____
_____
_____
_____
_____
_____
_____

Date [   ]

My Goal for today

_____

_____

To be the best you must be able to handle the worst.

_____

_____

_____

_____

Six most important things for today

1. _____

_____

_____

2. _____

_____

_____

3. _____

_____

_____

4. _____

_____

_____

5. _____

_____

_____

6. _____

_____

_____

My quote of the day

_____

_____

_____

_____

_____

_____

I AM.......

_____

_____

_____

_____

_____

_____

_____

_____

_____

_____

DAILY EVALUATION

My life is constantly under construction,
there is always something to improve!

_____ I read aloud my <u>Begin with the End in Mind</u> statement.

_____ I accomplished my six most important things list.

_____ I accomplished my goal for today.

_____ I read my book for the minutes I committed to.

_____ I listened to my motivational audio.

_____ I sat quietly and visualized my goal for ten minutes.

_____ I stayed on track with my new habit

What were my success's today?

_____

_____

_____

_____

_____

_____

_____

What will I do differently tomorrow?

_____

_____

_____

_____

_____

_____

_____

Date [   ]   **My Goal for today**

_____
_____
"You will see it when you believe it"   _____
                            Wayne Dyer   _____
_____
_____

Six most important things for today	My quote of the day
1. _____	_____
_____	_____
_____	_____
2. _____	_____
_____	_____
_____	_____
3. _____	
_____	**I AM.......**
_____	_____
4. _____	_____
_____	_____
_____	_____
5. _____	_____
_____	_____
_____	_____
6. _____	_____
_____	_____
_____	_____

DAILY EVALUATION

"Skill to do comes of doing."
Ralph Waldo Emerson

_____ I read aloud my <u>Begin with the End in Mind</u> statement.

_____ I accomplished my six most important things list.

_____ I accomplished my goal for today.

_____ I read my book for the minutes I committed to.

_____ I listened to my motivational audio.

_____ I sat quietly and visualized my goal for ten minutes.

_____ I stayed on track with my new habit

What were my success's today?

_____
_____
_____
_____
_____
_____
_____

What will I do differently tomorrow?

_____
_____
_____
_____
_____
_____
_____

Date [   ]   **My Goal for today**

_____

_____

"If everything seems under control,   _____
You're not going fast enough"
_____
Mario Andretti
_____

_____

Six most important things for today | **_My quote of the day_**

1. _____   _____

_____   _____

_____   _____

2. _____   _____

_____   _____

_____   _____

3. _____   **I AM.......**

_____   _____

_____   _____

4. _____   _____

_____   _____

_____   _____

5. _____   _____

_____   _____

_____   _____

6. _____   _____

_____   _____

_____   _____

DAILY EVALUATION

"Men can starve from a lack of self-realization as much as they can a lack of bread"

_____ I read aloud my <u>Begin with the End in Mind</u> statement.

_____ I accomplished my six most important things list.

_____ I accomplished my goal for today.

_____ I read my book for the minutes I committed to.

_____ I listened to my motivational audio.

_____ I sat quietly and visualized my goal for ten minutes.

_____ I stayed on track with my new habit

What were my success's today?

_____

_____

_____

_____

_____

_____

_____

What will I do differently tomorrow?

_____

_____

_____

_____

_____

_____

_____

Date [   ]   **My Goal for today**

_____

_____

"If opportunity doesn't knock, build   _____
a door"
_____

Milton Berle   _____

_____

Six most important things for today	My quote of the day
1. _____	_____
_____	_____
_____	_____
2. _____	_____
_____	_____
_____	_____
3. _____	
_____	**I AM.......**
_____	_____
4. _____	_____
_____	_____
_____	_____
5. _____	_____
_____	_____
_____	_____
6. _____	_____
_____	_____
_____	_____

200

DAILY EVALUATION

*"I think self-awareness is probably the most important
thing towards being a champion."*
Billie Jean King

_____ I read aloud my Begin with the End in Mind statement.

_____ I accomplished my six most important things list.

_____ I accomplished my goal for today.

_____ I read my book for the minutes I committed to.

_____ I listened to my motivational audio.

_____ I sat quietly and visualized my goal for ten minutes.

_____ I stayed on track with my new habit

What were my success's today?

_____

_____

_____

_____

_____

_____

_____

What will I do differently tomorrow?

_____

_____

_____

_____

_____

_____

_____

_____

Date [   ]

My Goal for today

_____
_____
_____

Today is the beginning of whatever you want!

_____
_____
_____
_____

Six most important things for today

1. _____
   _____
   _____

2. _____
   _____
   _____

3. _____
   _____
   _____

4. _____
   _____
   _____

5. _____
   _____
   _____

6. _____
   _____
   _____

My quote of the day

_____
_____
_____
_____
_____
_____

I AM.......

_____
_____
_____
_____
_____
_____
_____
_____
_____
_____

DAILY EVALUATION

*"Eventually people will realize that mistakes
are meant for learning not repeating"*

_____ I read aloud my <u>Begin with the End in Mind</u> statement.

_____ I accomplished my six most important things list.

_____ I accomplished my goal for today.

_____ I read my book for the minutes I committed to.

_____ I listened to my motivational audio.

_____ I sat quietly and visualized my goal for ten minutes.

_____ I stayed on track with my new habit

What were my success's today?

_____
_____
_____
_____
_____
_____
_____

What will I do differently tomorrow?

_____
_____
_____
_____
_____
_____
_____

DO THIS WEEKLY

How's it going? Jot down your thoughts and feelings in the spaces provided.

What are your feelings about the habit you are changing and the habit you are replacing it with?

_____

_____

_____

_____

_____

_____

_____

_____

_____

_____

Have you been able to stay on track with the new habit   YES   NO

Why?

_____

_____

_____

_____

_____

_____

_____

_____

_____

WEEKLY GAME PLAN

Target

_____

_____

_____

Day 1 objective

_____

Day 2

_____

Day 3

_____

Day 4

_____

Day 5

_____

Day 6

_____

Day 7

_____

DO THIS WEEKLY

Habit _____   <u>Positive</u>   <u>Negative</u>

                                                      _____   _____

                                                      _____   _____

                                                      _____   _____

                                                      _____   _____

                                                      _____   _____

Do the positives outweigh the negatives?

_____

Do I want to get rid of this habit?

_____

What are resources I have to help me?

_____

Replacement habit

_____

_____

Keys to success!

1. **Focus on what you want.**
2. **Reward yourself for staying on track.**
3. **Visualize yourself living life with the new habit firmly in place.**

REPETITION IS THE KEY!!!!

NOTES

Gratitude (What are you grateful for?)

1. _____

2. _____

3. _____

4. _____

5. _____

6. _____

7. _____

8. _____

9. _____

10. _____

Date [   ]   **My Goal for today**

_____
_____
"A comfort zone is a beautiful place   _____
but Nothing ever grows there"   _____
_____
_____

Six most important things for today	*My quote of the day*
1. _____	_____
_____	_____
_____	_____
2. _____	_____
_____	_____
_____	_____
3. _____	
_____	**I AM.......**
_____	_____
4. _____	_____
_____	_____
_____	_____
5. _____	_____
_____	_____
_____	_____
6. _____	_____
_____	_____
_____	_____

DAILY EVALUATION

*You can't have a million dollar dream with
a minimum wage work ethic*

____ I read aloud my <u>Begin with the End in Mind</u> statement.

____ I accomplished my six most important things list.

____ I accomplished my goal for today.

____ I read my book for the minutes I committed to.

____ I listened to my motivational audio.

____ I sat quietly and visualized my goal for ten minutes.

____ I stayed on track with my new habit

What were my success's today?
_____
_____
_____
_____
_____
_____
_____

What will I do differently tomorrow?
_____
_____
_____
_____
_____
_____
_____

Date [   ]   **My Goal for today**

_____

_____

"Life is 10% what happens to you and   _____
90% how you react to it"
_____

_____

_____

<u>Six most important things for today</u>

1. _____
   _____
   _____

2. _____
   _____
   _____

3. _____
   _____
   _____

4. _____
   _____
   _____

5. _____
   _____
   _____

6. _____
   _____
   _____

My quote of the day

_____

_____

_____

_____

_____

_____

I AM.......

_____

_____

_____

_____

_____

_____

_____

_____

_____

_____

DAILY EVALUATION

"Don't stop when you are tired, stop when you are done."

_____ I read aloud my <u>Begin with the End in Mind</u> statement.

_____ I accomplished my six most important things list.

_____ I accomplished my goal for today.

_____ I read my book for the minutes I committed to.

_____ I listened to my motivational audio.

_____ I sat quietly and visualized my goal for ten minutes.

_____ I stayed on track with my new habit

What were my success's today?

_____

_____

_____

_____

_____

_____

_____

What will I do differently tomorrow?

_____

_____

_____

_____

_____

_____

_____

Date [   ]   **My Goal for today**

_____

_____

Rule #1   _____

Never be #2   _____

_____

_____

Six most important things for today | ***My quote of the day***

1. _____   _____

_____   _____

_____   _____

2. _____   _____

_____   _____

_____   _____

3. _____

_____

_____   I AM.......

4. _____   _____

_____   _____

_____   _____

5. _____   _____

_____   _____

_____   _____

6. _____   _____

_____   _____

_____   _____

DAILY EVALUATION

The past cannot be changed, the future is yet in your power

_____ I read aloud my <u>Begin with the End in Mind</u> statement.

_____ I accomplished my six most important things list.

_____ I accomplished my goal for today.

_____ I read my book for the minutes I committed to.

_____ I listened to my motivational audio.

_____ I sat quietly and visualized my goal for ten minutes.

_____ I stayed on track with my new habit

What were my success's today?

_____
_____
_____
_____
_____
_____
_____

What will I do differently tomorrow?

_____
_____
_____
_____
_____
_____
_____

Date [   ]   **My Goal for today**

_____

_____

_____

"Success is the progressive realization   _____
of a Worthy goal or dream"
                                                _____
                    Earl Nightingale
                                                _____

Six most important things for today | *My quote of the day*

1. _____   _____

   _____   _____

   _____   _____

2. _____   _____

   _____   _____

   _____   _____

3. _____   _____

   _____
                                       I AM…….
   _____

4. _____   _____

   _____   _____

   _____   _____

5. _____   _____

   _____   _____

   _____   _____

6. _____   _____

   _____   _____

   _____   _____

DAILY EVALUATION

Don't wait for the right opportunity. Create it.

_____ I read aloud my <u>Begin with the End in Mind</u> statement.

_____ I accomplished my six most important things list.

_____ I accomplished my goal for today.

_____ I read my book for the minutes I committed to.

_____ I listened to my motivational audio.

_____ I sat quietly and visualized my goal for ten minutes.

_____ I stayed on track with my new habit

What were my success's today?

_____

_____

_____

_____

_____

_____

_____

What will I do differently tomorrow?

_____

_____

_____

_____

_____

_____

_____

Date [   ]   **My Goal for today**

_____

_____

_____

"Either you run the day or the day   _____
runs you."
                                          _____
                                Jim Rohn
                                          _____

Six most important things for today | ***My quote of the day***

1. _____   _____
   _____   _____
   _____   _____
                                       _____
2. _____   _____
   _____   _____
   _____   _____

3. _____   I AM.......
   _____
   _____   _____
                                       _____
4. _____   _____
   _____   _____
   _____   _____
                                       _____
5. _____   _____
   _____   _____
   _____   _____
                                       _____
6. _____   _____
   _____   _____
   _____

216

DAILY EVALUATION

The expert in everything was once a beginner.

_____ I read aloud my <u>Begin with the End in Mind</u> statement.

_____ I accomplished my six most important things list.

_____ I accomplished my goal for today.

_____ I read my book for the minutes I committed to.

_____ I listened to my motivational audio.

_____ I sat quietly and visualized my goal for ten minutes.

_____ I stayed on track with my new habit

What were my success's today?

_____

_____

_____

_____

_____

_____

_____

What will I do differently tomorrow?

_____

_____

_____

_____

_____

_____

_____

Date [   ]

My Goal for today

_____

_____

_____

You get what you settle for!

_____

_____

_____

Six most important things for today

1. _____

   _____

   _____

2. _____

   _____

   _____

3. _____

   _____

   _____

4. _____

   _____

   _____

5. _____

   _____

   _____

6. _____

   _____

   _____

My quote of the day

_____

_____

_____

_____

_____

_____

I AM.......

_____

_____

_____

_____

_____

_____

_____

_____

_____

_____

_____

DAILY EVALUATION

Great things never come from a comfort zone.

_____ I read aloud my <u>Begin with the End in Mind</u> statement.

_____ I accomplished my six most important things list.

_____ I accomplished my goal for today.

_____ I read my book for the minutes I committed to.

_____ I listened to my motivational audio.

_____ I sat quietly and visualized my goal for ten minutes.

_____ I stayed on track with my new habit

What were my success's today?
_____
_____
_____
_____
_____
_____
_____

What will I do differently tomorrow?
_____
_____
_____
_____
_____
_____
_____

Date [   ]   **My Goal for today**

_____

_____

"We all walk in the dark and each of   _____
us Must learn to turn on his or her
own light"   _____

Earl Nightingale   _____

_____

Six most important things for today	My quote of the day
1. _____	_____
_____	_____
_____	_____
2. _____	_____
_____	_____
_____	_____
3. _____	_____
_____	
_____	**I AM……**
4. _____	_____
_____	_____
_____	_____
5. _____	_____
_____	_____
_____	_____
6. _____	_____
_____	_____
_____	_____

DAILY EVALUATION

We can't become what we want by remaining who we are.

_____ I read aloud my <u>Begin with the End in Mind</u> statement.

_____ I accomplished my six most important things list.

_____ I accomplished my goal for today.

_____ I read my book for the minutes I committed to.

_____ I listened to my motivational audio.

_____ I sat quietly and visualized my goal for ten minutes.

_____ I stayed on track with my new habit

What were my success's today?

_____

_____

_____

_____

_____

_____

_____

What will I do differently tomorrow?

_____

_____

_____

_____

_____

_____

_____

_____

DO THIS WEEKLY

How's it going? Jot down your thoughts and feelings in the spaces provided.

What are your feelings about the habit you are changing and the habit you are replacing it with?

_____

_____

_____

_____

_____

_____

_____

_____

_____

_____

Have you been able to stay on track with the new habit   YES   NO

Why?

_____

_____

_____

_____

_____

_____

_____

_____

_____

_____

WEEKLY GAME PLAN

Target

_____

_____

_____

Day 1 objective

_____

Day 2

_____

Day 3

_____

Day 4

_____

Day 5

_____

Day 6

_____

Day 7

_____

DO THIS WEEKLY

Habit _____   <u>Positive</u>   <u>Negative</u>

_____	_____
_____	_____
_____	_____
_____	_____
_____	_____

Do the positives outweigh the negatives?

_____

Do I want to get rid of this habit?

_____

What are resources I have to help me?

_____

Replacement habit

_____

_____

Keys to success!

1. **Focus on what you want.**
2. **Reward yourself for staying on track.**
3. **Visualize yourself living life with the new habit firmly in place.**

REPETITION IS THE KEY!!!!

NOTES

Gratitude (What are you grateful for?)

1. _____

2. _____

3. _____

4. _____

5. _____

6. _____

7. _____

8. _____

9. _____

10. _____

Date [   ]   **My Goal for today**

_____
_____

"Fear does not stop death, it stops   _____
life!"   _____
_____
_____

Six most important things for today

1. _____
   _____
   _____

2. _____
   _____
   _____

3. _____
   _____
   _____

4. _____
   _____
   _____

5. _____
   _____
   _____

6. _____
   _____
   _____

My quote of the day

_____
_____
_____
_____
_____
_____

I AM.......

_____
_____
_____
_____
_____
_____
_____
_____
_____
_____

DAILY EVALUATION

Your only limit is you!

_____ I read aloud my <u>Begin with the End in Mind</u> statement.

_____ I accomplished my six most important things list.

_____ I accomplished my goal for today.

_____ I read my book for the minutes I committed to.

_____ I listened to my motivational audio.

_____ I sat quietly and visualized my goal for ten minutes.

_____ I stayed on track with my new habit

What were my success's today?

_____
_____
_____
_____
_____
_____
_____

What will I do differently tomorrow?

_____
_____
_____
_____
_____
_____
_____

Date [   ]   **My Goal for today**

_____

_____

"We tend to live up to our expectations"   _____

Earl Nightingale   _____

_____

_____

Six most important things for today   *My quote of the day*

1. _____   _____

_____   _____

_____   _____

2. _____   _____

_____   _____

_____   _____

3. _____

_____   I AM.......

_____   _____

4. _____   _____

_____   _____

_____   _____

5. _____   _____

_____   _____

_____   _____

6. _____   _____

_____   _____

_____   _____

DAILY EVALUATION

"When Shit happens turn it into fertilizer"

_____ I read aloud my <u>Begin with the End in Mind</u> statement.

_____ I accomplished my six most important things list.

_____ I accomplished my goal for today.

_____ I read my book for the minutes I committed to.

_____ I listened to my motivational audio.

_____ I sat quietly and visualized my goal for ten minutes.

_____ I stayed on track with my new habit

What were my success's today?

_____
_____
_____
_____
_____
_____
_____

What will I do differently tomorrow?

_____
_____
_____
_____
_____
_____
_____
_____

Date [   ]   **My Goal for today**

_____

_____

"Your past does not equal your future"   _____
                                    Tony Robbins   _____

_____

_____

Six most important things for today	*My quote of the day*
1. _____ _____ _____ 2. _____ _____ _____ 3. _____ _____ _____ 4. _____ _____ _____ 5. _____ _____ _____ 6. _____ _____ _____	_____ _____ _____ _____ _____ _____ **I AM…….** _____ _____ _____ _____ _____ _____ _____ _____ _____

DAILY EVALUATION

"You will never find time for anything, you must make it."
Charles Buxton. M

_____ I read aloud my <u>Begin with the End in Mind</u> statement.

_____ I accomplished my six most important things list.

_____ I accomplished my goal for today.

_____ I read my book for the minutes I committed to.

_____ I listened to my motivational audio.

_____ I sat quietly and visualized my goal for ten minutes.

_____ I stayed on track with my new habit

What were my success's today?
_____
_____
_____
_____
_____
_____
_____

What will I do differently tomorrow?
_____
_____
_____
_____
_____
_____
_____
_____

Date [   ]

My Goal for today

_____
_____
_____
_____
_____
_____

"Winners make a habit of manufacturing their own positive expectations in advanceof the event."

Brian Tracy

Six most important things for today

1. _____
   _____
   _____

2. _____
   _____
   _____

3. _____
   _____
   _____

4. _____
   _____
   _____

5. _____
   _____
   _____

6. _____
   _____
   _____

My quote of the day

_____
_____
_____
_____
_____
_____

I AM…….

_____
_____
_____
_____
_____
_____
_____
_____
_____
_____
_____

DAILY EVALUATION

Your life is your story, write well, edit often.

_____ I read aloud my <u>Begin with the End in Mind</u> statement.

_____ I accomplished my six most important things list.

_____ I accomplished my goal for today.

_____ I read my book for the minutes I committed to.

_____ I listened to my motivational audio.

_____ I sat quietly and visualized my goal for ten minutes.

_____ I stayed on track with my new habit

What were my success's today?

_____

_____

_____

_____

_____

_____

_____

What will I do differently tomorrow?

_____

_____

_____

_____

_____

_____

_____

Date [   ]

My Goal for today

_____
_____
_____
_____
_____
_____

"If you do what you've always done, you will Get what you've always gotten."

Tony Robbins

<u>Six most important things for today</u>

1. _____
   _____
   _____

2. _____
   _____
   _____

3. _____
   _____
   _____

4. _____
   _____
   _____

5. _____
   _____
   _____

6. _____
   _____
   _____

My quote of the day

_____
_____
_____
_____
_____
_____

I AM…….

_____
_____
_____
_____
_____
_____
_____
_____
_____
_____
_____

DAILY EVALUATION

Don't let small minds convince you that your dreams are to big!

_____ I read aloud my <u>Begin with the End in Mind</u> statement.

_____ I accomplished my six most important things list.

_____ I accomplished my goal for today.

_____ I read my book for the minutes I committed to.

_____ I listened to my motivational audio.

_____ I sat quietly and visualized my goal for ten minutes.

_____ I stayed on track with my new habit

What were my success's today?

_____

_____

_____

_____

_____

_____

_____

What will I do differently tomorrow?

_____

_____

_____

_____

_____

_____

_____

_____

Date [   ]   **My Goal for today**

_____

"The big thing is that you know what   _____
You want"
_____

Earl Nightingale   _____

_____

_____

<u>Six most important things for today</u>

1. _____
   _____
   _____

2. _____
   _____
   _____

3. _____
   _____
   _____

4. _____
   _____
   _____

5. _____
   _____
   _____

6. _____
   _____
   _____

My quote of the day

_____
_____
_____
_____
_____
_____

I AM.......

_____
_____
_____
_____
_____
_____
_____
_____
_____
_____

DAILY EVALUATION

The grass is greener where you water it.

_____ I read aloud my <u>Begin with the End in Mind</u> statement.

_____ I accomplished my six most important things list.

_____ I accomplished my goal for today.

_____ I read my book for the minutes I committed to.

_____ I listened to my motivational audio.

_____ I sat quietly and visualized my goal for ten minutes.

_____ I stayed on track with my new habit

What were my success's today?

_____
_____
_____
_____
_____
_____
_____

What will I do differently tomorrow?

_____
_____
_____
_____
_____
_____
_____

Date ┌─────────────┐   **My Goal for today**
     └─────────────┘

     _____
     _____
"Be so good they can't ignore you"   _____
                        Steve Martin   _____
     _____
     _____

┌─────────────────────────────┐ ┌─────────────────────────────┐
│ Six most important things for today │ *My quote of the day*   │
│   │ │   │
│ 1. _____   │ │ _____   │
│   _____   │ │ _____   │
│   _____   │ │ _____   │
│   │ │ _____   │
│ 2. _____   │ │ _____   │
│   _____   │ │ _____   │
│   _____   │ │ _____   │
│   │ └─────────────────────────────┘
│ 3. _____   │
│   _____   │ ┌─────────────────────────────┐
│   _____   │ │ I AM.......   │
│   │ │   │
│ 4. _____   │ │ _____   │
│   _____   │ │ _____   │
│   _____   │ │ _____   │
│   │ │ _____   │
│ 5. _____   │ │ _____   │
│   _____   │ │ _____   │
│   _____   │ │ _____   │
│   │ │ _____   │
│ 6. _____   │ │ _____   │
│   _____   │ │ _____   │
│   _____   │ │ _____   │
└─────────────────────────────┘ └─────────────────────────────┘

DAILY EVALUATION

Go as long as you can and then take another step!

_____ I read aloud my <u>Begin with the End in Mind</u> statement.

_____ I accomplished my six most important things list.

_____ I accomplished my goal for today.

_____ I read my book for the minutes I committed to.

_____ I listened to my motivational audio.

_____ I sat quietly and visualized my goal for ten minutes.

_____ I stayed on track with my new habit

What were my success's today?

_____

_____

_____

_____

_____

_____

_____

What will I do differently tomorrow?

_____

_____

_____

_____

_____

_____

_____

_____

DO THIS WEEKLY

How's it going? Jot down your thoughts and feelings in the spaces provided.

What are your feelings about the habit you are changing and the habit you are replacing it with?

_____

_____

_____

_____

_____

_____

_____

_____

_____

_____

Have you been able to stay on track with the new habit   YES   NO

Why?

_____

_____

_____

_____

_____

_____

_____

_____

_____

WEEKLY GAME PLAN

Target

_____

_____

_____

Day 1 objective

_____

Day 2

_____

Day 3

_____

Day 4

_____

Day 5

_____

Day 6

_____

Day 7

_____

DO THIS WEEKLY

Habit _____   <u>Positive</u>   <u>Negative</u>

_____   _____

_____   _____

_____   _____

_____   _____

_____   _____

Do the positives outweigh the negatives?

_____

Do I want to get rid of this habit?

_____

What are resources I have to help me?

_____

Replacement habit

_____

_____

Keys to success!

1. **Focus on what you want.**
2. **Reward yourself for staying on track.**
3. **Visualize yourself living life with the new habit firmly in place.**

REPETITION IS THE KEY!!!!

NOTES

Gratitude **(What are you grateful for?)**

1. _____

2. _____

3. _____

4. _____

5. _____

6. _____

7. _____

8. _____

9. _____

10. _____

Date [   ]   **My Goal for today**

_____

_____

"Don't wait for the perfect moment,   _____
take the moment and make it perfect."
_____

_____

_____

Six most important things for today	*My quote of the day*
1. _____	_____
_____	_____
_____	_____
2. _____	_____
_____	_____
_____	_____
3. _____	_____
_____	
_____	
4. _____	**I AM…….**
_____	_____
_____	_____
5. _____	_____
_____	_____
_____	_____
6. _____	_____
_____	_____
_____	_____

DAILY EVALUATION

Be better than you were yesterday

_____ I read aloud my <u>Begin with the End in Mind</u> statement.

_____ I accomplished my six most important things list.

_____ I accomplished my goal for today.

_____ I read my book for the minutes I committed to.

_____ I listened to my motivational audio.

_____ I sat quietly and visualized my goal for ten minutes.

_____ I stayed on track with my new habit

What were my success's today?

_____

_____

_____

_____

_____

_____

What will I do differently tomorrow?

_____

_____

_____

_____

_____

_____

_____

Date [   ]

My Goal for today

_____

_____

_____

You attract what you are not what you want, If you want great, then be great!

_____

_____

_____

_____

Six most important things for today

1. _____
   _____
   _____

2. _____
   _____
   _____

3. _____
   _____
   _____

4. _____
   _____
   _____

5. _____
   _____
   _____

6. _____
   _____
   _____

My quote of the day

_____

_____

_____

_____

_____

_____

I AM.......

_____

_____

_____

_____

_____

_____

_____

_____

_____

_____

_____

_____

DAILY EVALUATION

"It's easy to be a critic, but being a doer requires effort, risk, and change."
Wayne Dyer

_____ I read aloud my <u>Begin with the End in Mind</u> statement.

_____ I accomplished my six most important things list.

_____ I accomplished my goal for today.

_____ I read my book for the minutes I committed to.

_____ I listened to my motivational audio.

_____ I sat quietly and visualized my goal for ten minutes.

_____ I stayed on track with my new habit

What were my success's today?

_____
_____
_____
_____
_____
_____
_____

What will I do differently tomorrow?

_____
_____
_____
_____
_____
_____
_____

Date [   ]   **My Goal for today**

_____

_____

"It doesn't matter where you are   _____
coming from. All that matters is where   _____
you are going."   _____

Brian Tracy   _____

Six most important things for today	My quote of the day
1. _____	_____
_____	_____
_____	_____
2. _____	_____
_____	_____
_____	_____
3. _____	_____
_____	
_____	**I AM…….**
4. _____	_____
_____	_____
_____	_____
5. _____	_____
_____	_____
_____	_____
6. _____	_____
_____	_____
_____	_____

DAILY EVALUATION

Believe you can and you're half way there.

_____ I read aloud my <u>Begin with the End in Mind</u> statement.

_____ I accomplished my six most important things list.

_____ I accomplished my goal for today.

_____ I read my book for the minutes I committed to.

_____ I listened to my motivational audio.

_____ I sat quietly and visualized my goal for ten minutes.

_____ I stayed on track with my new habit

What were my success's today?

_____

_____

_____

_____

_____

_____

What will I do differently tomorrow?

_____

_____

_____

_____

_____

_____

_____

Date [   ]   **My Goal for today**

**"Never say anything about yourself
that you Don't want to come true."**
                              Brian Tracy

Six most important things for today

1. _____
   _____
   _____

2. _____
   _____
   _____

3. _____
   _____
   _____

4. _____
   _____
   _____

5. _____
   _____
   _____

6. _____
   _____
   _____

My quote of the day

I AM.......

DAILY EVALUATION

"An ounce of performance is worth pounds of promises"
Mae West

_____ I read aloud my <u>Begin with the End in Mind</u> statement.

_____ I accomplished my six most important things list.

_____ I accomplished my goal for today.

_____ I read my book for the minutes I committed to.

_____ I listened to my motivational audio.

_____ I sat quietly and visualized my goal for ten minutes.

_____ I stayed on track with my new habit

What were my success's today?
_____
_____
_____
_____
_____
_____
_____

What will I do differently tomorrow?
_____
_____
_____
_____
_____
_____
_____

Date [   ]   **My Goal for today**

_____

_____

"You'll find boredom where there is   _____
the absence of a good idea."
_____

_____

_____

Six most important things for today	My quote of the day
1. _____	_____
_____	_____
_____	_____
	_____
2. _____	_____
_____	_____
_____	
	I AM.......
3. _____	_____
_____	_____
_____	_____
	_____
4. _____	_____
_____	_____
_____	_____
	_____
5. _____	_____
_____	_____
_____	_____
	_____
6. _____	_____
_____	_____
_____	_____

DAILY EVALUATION

"The first and best victory is to conquer self"
Plato

_____ I read aloud my <u>Begin with the End in Mind</u> statement.

_____ I accomplished my six most important things list.

_____ I accomplished my goal for today.

_____ I read my book for the minutes I committed to.

_____ I listened to my motivational audio.

_____ I sat quietly and visualized my goal for ten minutes.

_____ I stayed on track with my new habit

What were my success's today?

_____

_____

_____

_____

_____

_____

_____

What will I do differently tomorrow?

_____

_____

_____

_____

_____

_____

_____

Date [   ]   **My Goal for today**

_____

_____

"Most people fail in life because they   _____
Major in minor things."
_____

Tony Robbins   _____

_____

Six most important things for today   _My quote of the day_

1. _____   _____

_____   _____

_____   _____

_____

2. _____   _____

_____   _____

_____

3. _____   I AM.......

_____   _____

_____   _____

4. _____   _____

_____   _____

_____   _____

_____

5. _____   _____

_____   _____

_____   _____

6. _____   _____

_____   _____

_____   _____

254

DAILY EVALUATION

Mistakes are proof that you are trying

_____ I read aloud my <u>Begin with the End in Mind</u> statement.

_____ I accomplished my six most important things list.

_____ I accomplished my goal for today.

_____ I read my book for the minutes I committed to.

_____ I listened to my motivational audio.

_____ I sat quietly and visualized my goal for ten minutes.

_____ I stayed on track with my new habit

What were my success's today?

_____

_____

_____

_____

_____

_____

_____

What will I do differently tomorrow?

_____

_____

_____

_____

_____

_____

_____

Date ┌─────────────────────┐ **My Goal for today**
     └─────────────────────┘

     _____

     _____

The best view comes after the hardest   _____
Climb.
     _____

     _____

     _____

┌──────────────────────────────┐ ┌──────────────────────────────┐
│ Six most important things for today │ │ *My quote of the day* │
│   │ │   │
│ 1. _____   │ │ _____   │
│   _____   │ │ _____   │
│   _____   │ │ _____   │
│   │ │ _____   │
│ 2. _____   │ │ _____   │
│   _____   │ │ _____   │
│   _____   │ │ _____   │
│   │ └──────────────────────────────┘
│ 3. _____   │
│   _____   │ ┌──────────────────────────────┐
│   _____   │ │ I AM……. │
│   │ │   │
│ 4. _____   │ │ _____   │
│   _____   │ │ _____   │
│   _____   │ │ _____   │
│   │ │ _____   │
│ 5. _____   │ │ _____   │
│   _____   │ │ _____   │
│   _____   │ │ _____   │
│   │ │ _____   │
│ 6. _____   │ │ _____   │
│   _____   │ │ _____   │
│   _____   │ │ _____   │
└──────────────────────────────┘ └──────────────────────────────┘

DAILY EVALUATION

You must do the thing you think you cannot

_____ I read aloud my <u>Begin with the End in Mind</u> statement.

_____ I accomplished my six most important things list.

_____ I accomplished my goal for today.

_____ I read my book for the minutes I committed to.

_____ I listened to my motivational audio.

_____ I sat quietly and visualized my goal for ten minutes.

_____ I stayed on track with my new habit

What were my success's today?

_____
_____
_____
_____
_____
_____
_____

What will I do differently tomorrow?

_____
_____
_____
_____
_____
_____
_____
_____

DO THIS WEEKLY

How's it going? Jot down your thoughts and feelings in the spaces provided.

What are your feelings about the habit you are changing and the habit you are replacing it with?

_____

_____

_____

_____

_____

_____

_____

_____

_____

_____

Have you been able to stay on track with the new habit   YES   NO

Why?

_____

_____

_____

_____

_____

_____

_____

_____

_____

_____

WEEKLY GAME PLAN

Target

_____

_____

_____

Day 1 objective

_____

Day 2

_____

Day 3

_____

Day 4

_____

Day 5

_____

Day 6

_____

Day 7

_____

DO THIS WEEKLY

Habit _____   <u>Positive</u>   <u>Negative</u>

_____   _____

_____   _____

_____   _____

_____   _____

_____   _____

Do the positives outweigh the negatives?

_____

Do I want to get rid of this habit?

_____

What are resources I have to help me?

_____

Replacement habit

_____

_____

Keys to success!

1. **Focus on what you want.**
2. **Reward yourself for staying on track.**
3. **Visualize yourself living life with the new habit firmly in place.**

REPETITION IS THE KEY!!!!

NOTES

Gratitude (What are you grateful for?)

1. _____

2. _____

3. _____

4. _____

5. _____

6. _____

7. _____

8. _____

9. _____

10. _____

Date

My Goal for today

_____
_____
_____
_____
_____
_____

Believe! Achieve! Succeed!

Six most important things for today

1. _____
   _____
   _____

2. _____
   _____
   _____

3. _____
   _____
   _____

4. _____
   _____
   _____

5. _____
   _____
   _____

6. _____
   _____
   _____

My quote of the day

_____
_____
_____
_____
_____
_____

I AM.......

_____
_____
_____
_____
_____
_____
_____
_____
_____
_____
_____

DAILY EVALUATION

It's never too late to be what you might have been

_____ I read aloud my <u>Begin with the End in Mind</u> statement.

_____ I accomplished my six most important things list.

_____ I accomplished my goal for today.

_____ I read my book for the minutes I committed to.

_____ I listened to my motivational audio.

_____ I sat quietly and visualized my goal for ten minutes.

_____ I stayed on track with my new habit

What were my success's today?

What will I do differently tomorrow?

Date [   ]   **My Goal for today**

_____
_____
"The mind moves in the direction of   _____
our Currently dominant thoughts"   _____
Earl Nightingale   _____
_____

Six most important things for today	*My quote of the day*

1. _____

_____

_____

2. _____

_____

_____

3. _____

_____

_____

4. _____

_____

_____

5. _____

_____

_____

6. _____

_____

_____

My quote of the day

_____
_____
_____
_____
_____
_____

I AM…….

_____
_____
_____
_____
_____
_____
_____
_____
_____
_____
_____

DAILY EVALUATION

"The key to success is action"
Brian Tracy

_____ I read aloud my <u>Begin with the End in Mind</u> statement.

_____ I accomplished my six most important things list.

_____ I accomplished my goal for today.

_____ I read my book for the minutes I committed to.

_____ I listened to my motivational audio.

_____ I sat quietly and visualized my goal for ten minutes.

_____ I stayed on track with my new habit

What were my success's today?

_____

_____

_____

_____

_____

_____

_____

What will I do differently tomorrow?

_____

_____

_____

_____

_____

_____

_____

Date [   ]   **My Goal for today**

                                 _____

"Your attitude, not your aptitude, will   _____
Determine you altitude."
                                 _____
                           Zig Zigler   _____

                                 _____

Six most important things for today	My quote of the day
1. _____	_____
_____	_____
_____	_____
2. _____	_____
_____	_____
_____	_____
3. _____	
_____	
_____	**I AM.......**
4. _____	_____
_____	_____
_____	_____
5. _____	_____
_____	_____
_____	_____
6. _____	_____
_____	_____
_____	_____

DAILY EVALUATION

"Most so called failures are only temporary defeats"
Napoleon Hill

_____ I read aloud my <u>Begin with the End in Mind</u> statement.

_____ I accomplished my six most important things list.

_____ I accomplished my goal for today.

_____ I read my book for the minutes I committed to.

_____ I listened to my motivational audio.

_____ I sat quietly and visualized my goal for ten minutes.

_____ I stayed on track with my new habit

What were my success's today?
_____
_____
_____
_____
_____
_____
_____

What will I do differently tomorrow?
_____
_____
_____
_____
_____
_____
_____

DO THIS WEEKLY

Habit _____   <u>Positive</u>   <u>Negative</u>

_____   _____

_____   _____

_____   _____

_____   _____

_____   _____

Do the positives outweigh the negatives?

_____

Do I want to get rid of this habit?

_____

What are resources I have to help me?

_____

Replacement habit

_____

_____

Keys to success!

1. **Focus on what you want.**
2. **Reward yourself for staying on track.**
3. **Visualize yourself living life with the new habit firmly in place.**

NOTES

Gratitude (What are you grateful for?)

1. _____

2. _____

3. _____

4. _____

5. _____

6. _____

7. _____

8. _____

9. _____

10. _____

Date _____

Monthly Reflection

What do you think went right this month?

What do you think went wrong?

Are your positive habits becoming easier?

Write down anything that will help you make better choices.

Make adjustments to your plan.

_____

_____

_____

_____

_____

_____

_____

_____

_____

_____

_____

_____

_____

_____

_____

_____

_____

_____

THE JOURNEY IS JUST BEGINNING

Congratulations on finishing this 3 month planner! The magic only continues if you continue! Hopefully you have given up some of your old habits that owned you and developed some new ones that are now serving you and bringing you closer to your goal/dream!

Continue to use your dream binder and visualizing time to bury your goal/ dream deeply into your miraculous subconscious mind and your goal will start to move at amazing speed to find you!

THE WORLD IS YOURS

WEEKLY GAME PLAN

Target

_____

_____

_____

Day 1 objective

_____

Day 2

_____

Day 3

_____

Day 4

_____

Day 5

_____

Day 6

_____

Day 7

_____

Habit _____   <u>Positive</u>   <u>Negative</u>

_____   _____
_____   _____
_____   _____
_____   _____
_____   _____

Do the positives outweigh the negatives?
_____

Do I want to get rid of this habit?
_____

What are resources I have to help me?
_____

Replacement habit or action
_____

Habit _____   <u>Positive</u>   <u>Negative</u>

_____   _____
_____   _____
_____   _____
_____   _____
_____   _____

Do the positives outweigh the negatives?
_____

Do I want to get rid of this habit?
_____

What are resources I have to help me?
_____

Replacement habit
_____

Habit: _____

        Own You_____   Serve You_____

Habit: _____

        Own You_____   Serve You_____

Habit: _____

        Own You_____   Serve You_____

Habit: _____

        Own You_____   Serve You_____

Habit: _____

        Own You_____   Serve You_____

Details make the difference

Write down as many details about your dream or goal as possible. This may take a while, come back to this page and add more as they come to you. Details help to cement the dream as you see it into your subconscious mind.

_____

_____

_____

_____

_____

_____

_____

_____

_____

_____

_____

_____

_____

_____

_____

_____

_____

_____

_____

_____

BEGIN WITH THE END IN MIND

Universal Subconscious Mind

_____

_____

Date_____

Pay to the order

of _____

_____Dollars

$ [   ]

Memo: _____

Universal Subconscious Mind

Universal Subconscious Mind

_____

_____

Date_____

Pay to the order

of _____

_____Dollars

$ [   ]

Memo: _____

Universal Subconscious Mind

_____

_____

_____

Date_____

Pay to the order
of _____

_____Dollars

$ [   ]

Memo: _____

_____

_____

_____

Date_____

Pay to the order
of _____

_____Dollars

$ [   ]

Memo: _____

278

Printed in the United States
by Baker & Taylor Publisher Services